Acclaim for Dr. Crawford's "Life from the Top of the Mind" System

"Dr. Bill is phenomenal! He is an excellent author and public speaker who provides scientific information as to how and why we operate from the top of the mind. I would recommend all material from Bill, as well as attending a live engagement. I have used his research in my personal and professional life and will continue to be refreshed on the topic with his continued support via monthly videos & empowering quotes.
Amazon Customer - July 24, 2018

"I have been to several of Dr. Bill's seminars, read this book, and recommended it to many of my clients. When they have applied what Dr. Bill teaches it has changed their organizations forever, making them more efficient, easier to do business with, and ultimately more profitable. And, by the way, a more enjoyable place to work!"
Amazon Customer - August 24, 2018

"I was fortunate enough to see Dr. Crawford speak at an executive conference and was immediately impressed with his methods of teaching his findings. We soon booked him to speak at our company to key management, and after hearing his content twice, wanted to own it. His books fill in all the blanks and expand on his material greatly. Hearing Dr. Crawford speak was certainly a great complement to his books. I also recommend his YouTube channel for great clips on specific topics."
Amazon Customer - July 31, 2018

"I have been to several of Dr. Crawford's seminars and his books have changed the way I think and react in virtually all situations. His easy way of relaying the information keeps you interested and informed. I refer to his books many times during my work in coaching and mentoring others".

Amazon Customer - May 22, 2018

"My company invited Dr. Bill for a group seminar and one on one sessions with each of our managers. The group session was extremely enlightening and the one-on-one time with Dr, Bill was invaluable to me and to our company. Subsequent to the aforementioned sessions, I have reached out to Dr. Bill regarding some personal matters and he has been very helpful.

I HIGHLY recommend that you read Dr. Bill's books, watch his videos, and if you get a chance, do yourself a favor and attend one of his Life from the Top of the Mind seminars."

Amazon Customer - April 10, 2018

"Life can be challenging - and so much surrounds communication and how we handle things. Dr. Bill shows us how to be better parents, friends, family and colleagues. I highly recommend his books - so many great takeaways!"

Amazon Customer - April 30, 2018

"I attended a half day seminar with Dr. Bill Crawford. It was amazing. Perhaps some of the most important material that we can learn. I really think that colleges and schools should include this content for managing life. It's really valuable in improving relationships, becoming more successful at home and at work, and being more mindful in our communication. I highly recommend his

books, and if you get the chance, listen to him in person!"
Amazon Customer - March 13, 2018

"Dr. Crawford has outdone himself with this book! If you have ever attended one of his seminars, you would know that he is passionate about helping and connecting with people. The information in "Life From The Top of the Mind" has useful, doable practices and advice that can be utilized in every stage of life! I strongly recommend this great read, and all his books! You will find yourself a better person for it!"
Amazon Customer - March 13, 2018

"I've had the pleasure of being in one of Dr. Crawford's classes. His high energy is infectious and so is the book. His books are beyond powerful for anyone that wants to understand how to reduce stress in your life and communicate better with others."
Amazon Customer - Feb. 26, 2018

"I love his *Life from the Top of the Mind* system! It's refreshing and exciting how Dr. Crawford delivers this simple but powerful, life-changing message. The more people get a handle on his books, the better the world will be. I feel blessed having found him and his work... lighter and way less stressed. :)
Amazon Customer - Dec. 12, 2017

For more "reviews" on Dr. Crawford and his work please visit https://www.billcrawfordphd.com/reviews/

WHAT TO SAY

WHAT TO SAY

And What Not To Say When...

Bill Crawford, Ph.D.

Florence Publishing
Houston, Tx

Copyright © 2019 Bill Crawford, Ph.D.

Manufactured in the United States of America
Text Graphics: Created by Bill Crawford and Georgia Crawford.
ISBN: 978-0-692-19313-6

Bill Crawford, Ph.D.
Crawford Performance Solutions
1-832-722-6147
Email - DrBill@BillCrawfordPhD.com
Website - www.BillCrawfordPhD.com

🖋*Florence Publishing*
Houston, Tx

To my wife Georgia,
and my sons,
Christopher and Nicholas
with all my love.

Acknowledgments

Each time I attempt a project as all-encompassing as writing a book, I am reminded of how much the talents and contributions of others play an integral part in creating the final product. I am grateful for the opportunity to thank these individuals for their support.

Let me begin close to home and start by thanking my wife, Georgia, for her support, patience, and enthusiasm for this project. Georgia did a wonderful job proofing and making changes in the final manuscript. I am continually amazed at how having her as a relationship partner has enriched my life and allowed me to do the work that I do from a foundation of love. Further, not only has she been a significant factor in the creation of this foundation, she continues to be an example of the power of love as a resource for re-creating a sense of family on a daily basis.

Let me also thank my two sons, Christopher and Nicholas. They continue to be a reminder of the importance of being purposeful in my role as a father so that I am always mindful of responding to life in a way I would be proud for them to emulate. This book, as well as, everything else I do, is dedicated to Georgia, Christopher, and Nicholas, with all my love.

I would also like to thank all the workshop participants and clients who have repeatedly asked for a book such as this, and given me so many wonderful examples of the type of situations in which knowing what to say is so important.

And, finally, I would like to thank my mother and father, Florence and Burton Crawford. Even though they passed away almost 40 years ago, I am touched daily by their warmth, love, and philosophy of life. Their commitment to creating a loving home for me, as well as, helping others through the programs of A.A. and Alanon has given me a foundation on which to build a life and a life's work. In many ways, they live on in every word of this book.

Contents

Section I - Life in General

*Chapter 1 - What to Say…When There is a History
of Conflict &/or Misunderstanding*   *31*

*Chapter 2 - What to Say…When Someone is Accusing
You of Something You Didn't Do*   *35*

*Chapter 3 - What to Say…When Someone is Asking
You a Question You Don't Want to Answer*   *41*

*Chapter 4 - What to Say… When Someone is Accusing
You of Not Listening or Not Understanding*   *45*

*Chapter 5 - What to Say… When Someone has Lost a
Loved One*   *49*

*Chapter 6 - What to Say…When Your Family Member,
Child, or Supervisor Has Made a Mistake*   *53*

*Chapter 7 - What to Say…When Someone is Gossiping
About You At Work*   *57*

Section II - Business

*Chapter 8 - What to Say…When You are Giving Negative
Feedback in a Performance Review*   *63*

Chapter 9 - What to Say…When There is Conflict
        Between Two of Your Employees   67

Chapter 10 - What to Say…When You are
        Interviewing for a Job   71

Chapter 11 - What to Say…When Your Managers
        Aren't Working Well with Others   75

Chapter 12 - What to Say…When you Have Tried
        Everything but Nothing Works
        (The Nuclear Option)   79

Chapter 13 - What to Say…When Your Customer
        Is Making Unreasonable Demands   85

Chapter 14 - What to Say…When you Want a Raise   89

Section III - Friends and Family

Chapter 15 - What to Say…When Your Friends Keep
        Coming to You with Their Troubles   95

Chapter 16 - What to Say…When your Toddler
        is Throwing a Tantrum   99

Chapter 17 - What to Say…When Your Parents
        Aren't Supporting Your Dreams   105

Chapter 18 - What to Say…When Your Ex Is
        Being a Jerk!   113

Chapter 19 - What to Say…When Your Parents
        are Still Treating You Like a Child   115

Chapter 20 - What to Say… When Someone is
        Trying to Make You Feel Guilty   119

*Chapter 21 - What to Say…When Your Aging
Parents Won't Listen To Your Advice* 123

*Chapter 22 -What to Say…When You Want to Heal
a Broken Relationship with Friends
or Family* 129

*Chapter 23 - What to say…When You Want to Stop
Becoming Frustrated at Family
Gatherings* 133

*Chapter 24 - What to Say…When You Want Your
Children to Go to Bed* 137

*Chapter 25 - What to Say…When Your Child Seems
to Be Anxious about Everything* 143

*Chapter 26 - What to Say…When Your Teenager
Seems to Ignore You, or Won't Cooperate
with You, In General* 149

Section Part IV - Relationships

*Chapter 27 - What to Say…When There Are Problems
in Your Relationship* 157

*Chapter 28 - What to Say…When You Want To
Break Up* 163

*Chapter 29 - What to Say …When Your Child (or
Family Member) Comes Out as LGBTQ* 169

Section Part V - The Formula

*Chapter 30 - The LEAP Model, or the "What to Say"
Formula* 177

What To Say

Introduction (Read Me First!)

I must admit that I was a bit hesitant to write this book. You see, while I do believe in the power of words to work out a disagreement, heal a relationship, or right a wrong, I have always tried to tell those who asked me about "what to say" that it is never really about specific words, but rather about the intent behind the words and being authentic. Plus, the context of the conversation always plays an important role in how things are said. We talk to family members differently from how we talk to business associates, and we talk to our bosses differently than we talk to those we supervise, or to our kids.

Further, I have been concerned that if people were worried that they had to say things exactly the right way, they would become self-conscious and, thus, less effective. However, what I hear over and over from both my clients and those who participate in my seminars, is that they want my suggestions on how to frame what they want to say so that they are truly understood, and for that reason, I have decided to give you my best thoughts on the subject.

As I think back, this is actually something that I was able to do as a child. In my neighborhood, one thing that my friends and I loved to do was sleep over at each other's houses, and we tried to make this happen as often as possible. The challenge was how to get our parents (meaning mostly our mothers) to agree to this. For some reason, I was always chosen as the person to convince the "powers that be" to grant these wishes, and I remember both enjoying this role, and being supremely confident that I could pull it off.

As I matured and began to study psychology, this ability to know what to say also matured through my exposure to theories of human behavior. Eventually, I began to create my own theory of success and happiness based upon the latest brain science. In fact, my system, that I call "Life from the Top of the Mind," has a component on how to talk to those who are resistant to your message, and it is one of the more popular aspects of my seminars.

As a result of this popularity, and at the urging of some of my close friends and clients, I have decided to bring this scientific perspective to you in the form of this book. In other words, I'm not just giving "advice" here, but using the latest brain science to help you frame what you want to say so that it has the maximum impact. Basically, this means that in order to communicate effectively, we need to understand what part of the brain we are coming from and how to get others to shift from their resistant brain to their receptive brain.

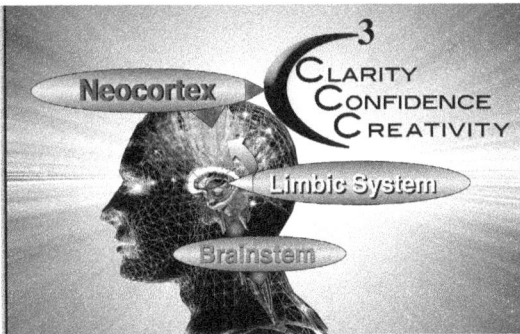

The resistant brain is the lower 20% of the brain, or the brainstem. This is where our fight-or-flight responses are located, and when those we are wanting to influence are stuck in this lower brain, just "telling it like it is" won't work. Neither will trying to be logical with them (at least initially), or trying to convince them that we are right, because they are coming from the part of the brain that is illogical, and ruled by predominantly negative emotions. They are afraid that we don't understand and are just trying to convince them that they are wrong. Unfortunately, when we are stuck in this resistant brain as well, we then tend to think the same about them.

Frankly, this is the reason there are so many problems and conflict in communication. Often, everyone is feeling misunderstood and reacting emotionally, trying to convince the "other" of the righteousness of their perspective.

Therefore, to be influential with others, two things must happen. First, we must be coming from the "Top of the Mind." This is the purposeful (versus reactive) upper 80% of the brain called the neocortex. This means that we need to be clear, confident, and creative with respect to our communication.

For those wanting a system of how to shift from the brainstem (what I will refer to in this book as the "lower brain") to the neocortex (or the "Top of the Mind") in order to choose our thoughts, emotions, and words more purposefully, I encourage you to check out my book,

"Life From The Top Of The Mind."

Second, we must know "what to say," or how to communicate in a way that takes what is important to them and blends their perspective with what is important to us so that they hear our words as valuable. Of course, to do this, we must know what is important to them and how it fits with what is important to us. This is why listening is always taught as one of the critical steps of communication and influence. When we listen, we learn the key to their cooperation because we learn what is important to them and/or what they are concerned about.

This reminds me of one of my favorite quotes, "Wisdom is the reward we get for listening all of those times we would have preferred to talk." (Adapted from Doug Larson). In other words, until we know what is important to them, we won't know how to frame our communication in a way that leads to mutual understanding and/or a mutually-agreed upon solution.

Of course, knowing what to say at the beginning of the interaction, or how to start the conversation so that they are open to talking with us is also critical, and, therefore, I will be giving you my best thoughts on this as well. Just

remember that this isn't about how to manipulate others or trick them in to agreeing with
you. In order to use this information effectively, you must be sincere in your desire to create
a solution that benefits all concerned.

Therefore, we must constantly ask ourselves
a very important question...how can I frame
what I have to say in a way that others will
hear as valuable? This will be a critical component to successful communication in all the
examples we explore, so be sure to keep it in
mind as I give you suggestions on what to say
in different situations.

To be clear, I am not saying that these suggestions are the only ways to communicate effectively. Plus, in order to cover as much ground
as possible, I have chosen to be brief. We all
know that human interactions are complicat-
ed, and it's possible that each scenario could
be a book in and of themselves. These are just
my best thoughts on what I believe to be the
most common situations based upon my training and experience.

Therefore, rather than worry about whether
you would have said it this way, I suggest that
you pay particular attention to how my words
resonate with you. Do they make sense? Can

you see why I would suggest saying things this way? Remember, while I will be giving you specifics on "what to say" that I believe will help you communicate with others more successfully, I don't want you to become robotic or inauthentic. Therefore, feel free to take any of my suggestions, and change them to fit your personality and communication style.

The good news is that you are already one step ahead of the game. In other words, the fact that you are interested in communicating in the most effective way is half the battle, because it means that you are giving serious thought to this important aspect of interpersonal interaction.

As to how to navigate through the book, you will find that the material is divided into sections covering broad categories such as family, business, and relationships, as well as a general category where the specific situation could occur almost anywhere. Within these broad categories, there will be specific chapters focusing on specific situations. For example, what to say when someone has lost a loved one, when you want your children to cooperate with you, when your friend keeps coming to you with their troubles, when someone you supervise needs to improve their performance, and so on.

Regardless of where you start, however, I would encourage you to also read the last chapter (Chapter 30- The LEAP Model, or the "What To Say" Formula) because here I lay out my "formula" for successful communication, with the goal of giving you a way of thinking about "what to say" in future situations.

Within each chapter, I have divided my thoughts into:

• The Problem
• What <u>Not</u> to Say
• A "Top of the Mind" Solution (how to look at this situation from the clear, confident, and creative part of the brain).

And finally:

• What to Say (how to take everything we know and frame our thoughts in a way that leads to a mutually-beneficial solution.

You are certainly welcome to read the book cover to cover, however, now that you have been exposed to how the different parts of the brain affect communication, you may also simply turn to the sections or chapters that interest you.

My sincere hope is that you will find this information valuable and, as a result, you will become more influential in your life and in the lives of others by knowing what to say.

Section I
Life In General

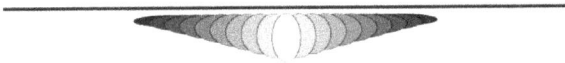

CHAPTER I

What to Say...
When There is a History
of Conflict &/or
Misunderstanding

The Problem

I'm sure that we have all experienced attempting to engage someone with whom we have a history of conflict. Whether this is a family member, a friend, or a business associate, this negative history colors how they see us, and, therefore, they are not likely to be particularly enthusiastic about, or open to any new conversation. As discussed in the introduction, they are coming from the resistant brain, and are probably viewing us with suspicion, if not outright hostility.

What Not to Say…

Chances are, if there has been conflict in the relationship in the past, you may be dreading the upcoming conversation, and/or feeling somewhat resentful that the other person is continuing to see you in such a negative light. I strongly suggest that you not allow those feelings of dread and resentment to color how you begin the conversation. In other words, I would not encourage you to just jump in to the discuss as if nothing has happened, or say something like,

Listen, we really have to get past the fact that we don't like each other.

While this does somewhat address the fact that there is a history of conflict, the potential that the other person would respond positively to that is small.

A Top of the Mind Solution

What you are wanting is to get to keep the past from continuing to negatively affect the present and future. Therefore, when you are dealing with a situation in which there is a history of conflict, you must address this history before any real communication can happen, and in a way that they will hear as valuable. Plus, chances are that they are thinking that you are going to continue to blame them for the problem.

What to Say…

I suggest that we address all of this by saying something like:

(Name of person), *I know we have had our differences in the past, and as I look back on these interactions, I'm not sure I have done the best job of truly understanding your perspective or what is important to you. Would you agree?*

The reason this has the potential to be more effective is that you are taking responsibility for your part of any past conflict, while, at the same time, laying a foundation for something different going forward. This isn't about you taking all of the blame, but rather just acknowledging that every conflict requires participation from at least two individuals, and you are taking responsibility for your part of the past.

You then can speak to why you are talking to them in this new way by addressing the importance of the relationship and create a vision for more productive conversations in the future. You could say something like:

Great, I know we both want our interactions to be more productive, (or loving, if you are talking to a family member) so if I take more responsibility for really listening to you and working to understand your perspective ... would you be willing to do that with me?

Now, here, they might say: "That's what I have been doing all along! YOU are the one who hasn't been listening!

I suggest that you look beyond the criticism, and stay focused on what you want, i.e., both of you doing a better job of understanding each other. This means that rather than criticizing them for criticizing you, you could just say something like:

I can see how that would have been frustrating, and... it sounds like we both want to discuss issues in the future in a way that has everyone feeling heard and understood.

Of course, you might say it differently. Just keep in mind that the goal here is to deal with past conflict in a way that allows for more productive and successful conversations in the future, and not to get into an argument about who was or is right or wrong.

CHAPTER 2

What to Say...
When Someone is
Accusing You of Something
You Didn't Do

The Problem

You are being accused of something you not only didn't do, but is also totally outside of your character. You feel insulted that someone could think that of you.

What Not to Say...

Unfortunately, telling them how hurt or insulted you feel because they have accused you of something like this will only have them defending their accusation.

Therefore, what you don't want to say is something like, "How dare you accuse me of something like that?"

A Top of the Mind Solution

What you are wanting is to get past this accusation so that you can deal with the underlying problem. This will require you to be in the clear, confident, creative part of your brain.

What to Say...

Therefore, rather than defending yourself or accusing your accuser of insulting you, I suggest you question the accusation by drawing on your character. In other words, if you know that what you're being accused of is not who you are, you could simply say something like:

Is that really congruent with who you know me to be?

Or...

Does that really fit with whom you know me to be?

This can have them rethinking their accusation in terms of whom they know you to be, and potentially realizing that they were mistaken in accusing you in the first place.

This happened to me when I was running a therapy group with a colleague. We wanted to do the group together because we enjoyed working with each other, plus, having two counselors as group leaders has the advantage of the group being covered in case the other isn't available for some reason. As it turned out, I began receiving numerous offers to speak out of town, and this caused me to miss several sessions.

My colleague must have felt taken advantage of because she confronted me with, "Hey Bill, are you trying to just dump this group on me?" I was able to gather my thoughts and respond with, "Is that congruent with who you know me to be?" She thought for a moment and said, "No." I then said, "Thank you. Now, let's look at the problem of my being away for so many sessions and come up with a solution that works for both of us."

Of course, it is certainly possible that the person accusing you isn't as aware or willing to rethink their accusation as my colleague was. In fact, it's possible that they may say, "Yes!" (meaning they do think that whatever they are accusing you of is congruent with who they know you to be). Here, it's once again important that you continue coming from the clear, confident, creative brain (the neocortex, or Top of the Mind) in which case you could say something like:

I see, so I'm curious, what have you seen me do in the past that would lead you to believe that I'm that sort of person?

Here, you are wanting to do two things: A) Once again, give them the opportunity to rethink their accusation, and B) if they still feel that you are indeed this sort of person, this question will help you understand why they seem to think of you in this way so that you can potentially address this original misconception. If they do give you a specific example, and you can see how they might have misinterpreted what was going on, you could say something like:

Oh, okay, that makes sense, I can see how you would be concerned about that…would you like to know what I was really thinking?

Remember, the key here is that you are being curious and addressing misunderstandings versus defending yourself or attacking the person who is accusing you. In other words, you are displaying characteristics that are congruent with a quality person versus someone who is guilty. Even if these conversations don't end in their apologizing for their accusation, chances are they will think twice about accusing you in the future because they know you will come from a place of character and curiosity.

Of course, if you have made choices in the past that you regret, and if what you are being accused of now is congruent with those mistakes, you could say something like,

Yes, based upon some of my behavior in the past, I can see how you would think of me in this way. I just want you to know that I have changed, and I encourage you to continue gathering information on who I am now and in the future. My hope is that as you see me becoming more purposeful in my choices, your opinion of me will change as well.

While chances are this won't have them immediately changing how they see you, it is very likely to shape how they interpret your behavior in the future because you have made them more aware of the changes you are making in your life.

CHAPTER 3

What to Say...
When Someone is
Asking A Question You
Don't Want To Answer

The Problem

You are being asked a question that either you haven't had time to consider, or simply don't want to answer. Unfortunately, most of us have been trained to believe that we must answer any question put to us (certainly this was the case when we were children and were being questioned by our parents or teachers), and, therefore, we tend to stumble, stutter, or say something we regret later.

What Not To Say...

In these situations, I encourage you not to attack the question or the questioner. In other words, reacting indignantly by challenging their "right" to ask you this sort of question will only make you look guilty.

A Top of the Mind Solution

What you are wanting is to respond in a way that allows you to choose when and if you want to answer the question.

What To Say...

I suggest that you respond with curiosity. For example, you could say something as simple as:

"Interesting question...what makes you ask?"

If the questioner's motives were nefarious, they will probably not know what to say because they can't really admit that they were trying to trap you or illicit a negative response. However, I think it's fair to say that sometimes people are just curious. They don't really think about the question before they ask it, and truly mean no harm.

This still doesn't mean that you have to answer. However, when you meet their question with curiosity, you accomplish several things. One, you may discover a motivation behind their question, or information that makes responding easier.

Of course, if they respond to your question with "just curious," you can still control when (and if) you answer by saying something like:

Okay, let me give it some thought, and if something comes to mind, I will get back to you.

Of course, the words "let me give it some thought" are not really asking them for their permission to think about their question. It simply gives you the power to respond when, and if you choose to sometime in the future.

The bottom line is that, as adults, we have the right to determine what questions we answer. When we are put on the defensive by questions we don't want to answer, chances are our defensiveness will have us responding in ways that are not productive.

Of course, if the motivation behind our choosing not to answer a question is shame, anxiety, or some fear that our answer will expose some aspect of our life that we are trying to hide, then this should be explored with someone we trust. We don't want to just use avoidance as a way to deal with problems that need our attention.

However, if we are clear that this is simply a question

in which the answer would be none of their business, or we don't really trust them to hear the answer in a way that solves a problem, then we can exercise our right as adults to choose whether to answer the question or not.

CHAPTER 4

What to Say...
When Someone is
Accusing You of Not
Listening or Understanding

The Problem

This generally occurs in the middle of a heated conversation when the two parties are engaged in a "who's right" debate, and where one or both feel attacked. Unfortunately, whether you are the accuser or the accused, responding more vehemently in a way that defends your position is unlikely to lead to a productive resolution.

What Not to Say...

Again, what you probably don't want to tell them is how wrong they are for accusing you of not listening, or try to give them examples of when you did listen. Basically, you don't want to defend yourself, because they are likely to attack your defense.

A Top of the Mind Solution

What you are wanting is to move beyond the debate about who's listening to whom, and then resolve the problem.

What to Say...

Therefore, I encourage you to take their accusation as good information about how they perceive you and use it to change the conversation. For example, you could say something like,

Oh, okay, so if I were interacting with you in a way where you felt heard and understood, what would I be doing differently?

This is what I call a neocortex question because it is about the future and the solution versus "who's right" in the past. Of course, when someone is upset and accusing you of not listening, chances are they are in their brainstem (the "upset" part of the brain). Therefore, when you ask them a neocortex question, it may actually take a moment for them to answer because, (1) they probably aren't expecting this sort of response, and (2) they have to shift to the neocortex to answer the question. Therefore, you will want to give them a second or two to respond.

They might still be a bit exasperated and say something like, "I don't know, just listen to me!!!"

To which you could respond with something like:

Okay, if I work hard at listening to you and really understanding what is important to you, would you be willing to do the same with me?

The key here is that you are changing their criticism from a problem to part of the solution by partnering with it and laying a foundation for a more productive way of interaction going forward.

CHAPTER 5

What to Say...
When Someone Has
Lost A Loved One

The Problem

Obviously, the person who has lost a loved one is dealing with a myriad of emotions from deep sadness to confusion, anger, anxiety, and maybe even guilt. Often, those around them see how bad they are feeling, and try to make them feel better.

What Not to Say...

While it's understandable that you want to help them feel better, this isn't what they need. Saying something like, "I'm sure (Name) is in a better place." or even the line we hear on every police show, "I'm sorry for your loss," may be well-intentioned, but it is unlikely to be helpful.

A Top of the Mind Solution

What you are wanting is to express your compassion and caring without implying that how they are dealing with the situation needs to change.

What to Say...

I suggest that you help them become more comfortable with their grief, no matter what form it takes. For example, in situations where someone has lost a loved one, the depth of their pain is very likely to match the depth of their love for the person who has died. Therefore, as a psychologist who regularly helps people deal with loss and grief, I suggest you say something like:

I can see how much you loved (Name) and I'm so sorry this happened. If there is anything I can do, please don't hesitate to ask.

As a speaker and corporate trainer who talks regularly about dealing with stress, my goal is to help people feel better and accomplish more by influencing how the brain processes information. However, as a psychologist (as well as a father, husband, and friend), I help people deal with loss and grief by helping them tie their tears (as well as the other intense emotions that accompany grief) to their love for the person they lost. This can give grieving new meaning and help make the process become the healing experience it is designed to be.

Unfortunately, our western culture tends to view grieving as our failure to cope. We call it "breaking down, losing it, falling to pieces," etc. This only makes the pain worse because we feel like failures for feeling these deep emotions.

However, if we can tie our grieving to our love (I call the tears of grief "liquid love,") we can be proud of how we feel, and allow these waves of emotion to wash over us, and then come out on the other side feeling just a little better.

In terms of helping others deal with loss, we just need to keep in mind that everyone does it in their own way. There is no "right or wrong" way to grieve. In fact, some helping professionals that regularly work with those in grief look at the early stages of shock and denial as necessary for some people to keep the deep pain at bay long enough to marshal internal and external resources.

Therefore, the more we can let people know that their

deep feelings are about how much they care and who they are (i.e., loving people who feel understandably bad when someone they love passes away), we can be a source of comfort in painful times.

CHAPTER 6

What to Say...
When a Family Member,
Your Child, or Supervisee
Has Made a Mistake

The Problem

Most of us have been taught that the way to help someone learn from a mistake or avoid making the same mistake again is to ensure that they feel bad about what they did. Therefore, when someone we care for or supervise makes a mistake, we tend to judge whether they have learned anything, at least initially, by how bad they feel. If we think that they are not feeling bad enough, we interpret that to mean that they are not taking the mistake seriously, and we try to make them feel bad.

This generally results in one of two reactions, shame or blame. However, because both shame and blame are lower brain (brainstem) responses (blame is fight, shame is flight), neither is particularly effective in promoting learning.

In fact, some people will actually use the feelings of guilt and shame as their penance. In other words, once they feel they have felt badly enough about the mistake, they will move on without any significant learning other than the desire to avoid getting caught in the future.

What Not to Say...

Therefore, what we don't want to do is say something like, "What were you thinking?" Or, with our kids, "How many times have we talked about this?" As a result, this will only have them stuck in the brainstem, feeling ashamed, and/or looking for someone to blame.

In fact, this is the problem with what many business leaders (and parents) see as a lack of accountability in today's workforce, and with today's youth. The truth is that people are reluctant to be "accountable," because, to them, this means who's to blame when something goes wrong.

A Top of the Mind Solution

What you are wanting is for them to learn from their mistake and apply that learning to future behavior.

What to Say...

Given what we discussed in the introduction in terms of how the brain processes data, we know that the best decisions (as well as the best learning) comes from the upper 80% of the brain, or the neocortex. Therefore, the best way to help someone learn from a mistake is ask to them a "neocortex question." This is a question that can only be asked and answered from the upper 80% of the brain, and almost always focuses on the future and the solution, versus the problem and the past.

Therefore, when someone has made a mistake, you could say something like:

Okay, knowing what you know now, how would you do that differently in the future?

Because there is no shame or blame in the future, they are likely to take what they have learned and apply it to some future behavior which is (a) the only time we can affect behavior, and (b) exactly what we want them to do.

Of course, they could also be afraid that there is

a certain "right answer" or worse, that they truly didn't learn anything from the mistake, in which case they might respond to the question "Knowing what you know now, how would you do that differently in the future?" with a sheepish, "I don't know." The good news is that you can still get them to start thinking in this more solution-focused way by saying something like:

No problem, I have some ideas. Let's kick them around and see what works.

Again, because you are talking about the future, the solution, and their success versus the problem and the past, they are likely to be more open to the discussion and learning what you want them to learn.

By the way, this is a great way to support ourselves in learning from our mistakes as well (versus getting caught in shame or blame). When we make a choice that doesn't create more problems than solutions, we can ask:

"Okay, knowing what I know now, how would I do this differently in the future?"

Chances are the answer will be good information!

CHAPTER 7

What to Say...
When Someone Is
Gossiping About You
At Work

The Problem

You are being talked about negatively by someone in your organization, and you may even know who it is. However, confronting them will almost always result in their denying any involvement and then going out and gossiping about you again.

What Not to Say...

I would not encourage you to try to educate them on the corporate policy on gossip, or to say something like: "Okay, I know you are the one who has been spreading lies about me, so STOP IT!"

A Top of the Mind Solution

What you are wanting is to engage the person who is gossiping in a way that they are less likely to do so in the future.

What To Say...

Therefore, I suggest you confront the issue without blaming them. In this case, you could say something like:

Did you know that there are people in this organization who actually go around talking negatively about others behind their back?

This puts the issue of gossip on the table without directly accusing them of the crime, and phrases the question in a way that implies how hard it is to believe that people would actually do something like this.

It's possible that they might then respond in an incredulous tone, with something like, "No way! Really??" To which you can reply,

It's true! Which is hard to understand because you know

that the gossip always gets back to the person being talked about.

Here you are letting them know that you know, but they will have difficulty getting defensive without admitting that they are the culprit.

Of course, if they do react defensively with something like, "Wait, are you accusing me of gossiping?" You can reply with,

No, of course not. You would never do something like that, would you?

Again, they are very likely to respond to this by agreeing with you. I mean, what choice do they have?

Now, whether this totally stops them from ever gossiping again is unlikely, and not really the point. Sadly, there are always going to be people who build themselves up and make themselves important to others by putting others down. What you have done, however, is put them on notice that their behavior has been noted, which may have them thinking twice before gossiping again… at least about you.

Of course, the best way to deal with gossipers is to just be who you are, and when your colleagues hear negative things about you, it will be so incongruent with who they know you to be that they are likely to reject the gossip outright. In this case, the negative comments will be more information about the person who is doing the gossiping than about you.

Section II
Business

CHAPTER 8

What to Say...
When You are Giving
Negative Feedback in a
Performance Review

The Problem

Many employees tend to interpret negative feedback in performance reviews as criticism and react defensively. Unfortunately, many supervisors then try to convince the employee of the validity of the negative feedback, which often results in the employee defending the very behavior they need to change.

What Not to Say...

When this happens, many managers or supervisors

double down on the righteousness of their perspective, and say something like, "Listen, I'm telling you this for your own good, and unless you are willing to change, you may need to find a different job!"

As you might imagine, this will tend to drive the employee deeper into the brainstem where, even if they agree to listen (because they don't want to lose their job), they will very likely leave the conversation full of anger and resentment.

A Top of the Mind Solution

What you are wanting is to be able to help the employee hear your feedback and change in a way that enhances their success.

What to Say...

Rather than trying to convince the employee that they are wrong, I suggest that you partner with the part of them that feels wrongly accused. To do this, we must be able to interpret their being upset as part of the solution versus part of the problem. I suggest that we do this by recognizing that this means that they care about how they are perceived by the organization. That's the good news!

To do this, you could say something like:

"You may be surprised to hear this, but I'm impressed with your being upset… it means that you care how you are perceived by the organization. You would not believe how some people react to this sort of feedback…it's almost as if they don't care.

Would it be fair to say that you feel misunderstood, as if the organization isn't seeing you as the valuable employee you know yourself to be?

The employee will most likely answer in the affirmative, to which you can reply:

"That makes sense, so how about we put our heads together and see what you can do to have more influence in how you are perceived? Sound good?"

Again, the employee is likely to agree with this, and you have changed how they see you from an accuser to an ally. You can now begin to help them change the behavior that has resulted in their being perceived in a negative light. This means that you have also changed how they interpret your suggestions for improvement, which means that they are now more likely to change what needs to be changed.

Of course, sometimes even this unique approach doesn't result in the changes you were looking for. When this happens, check out information in Chapter 12 (What to Say… When Nothing Works.)

CHAPTER 9

What to Say...
When There is Conflict
Between Two of Your
Employees

The Problem

Two of your employees are embroiled in conflict that not only limits their productivity but seems to put you in the middle of the conflict in the role of referee or judge.

What Not to Say...

Unlike parents who are dealing with fights between their children, I don't suggest you say: "You two need to figure this out and learn how to work together!" The reason this tactic rarely works is that both employees are coming from their brainstems, which means that they are reacting emotionally versus rationally.

A Top of the Mind Solution

What you are wanting is for each person to take more responsibility for how they are reacting, and learn how to work with all types of people.

What to Say...

In cases like this, you first have to tap into the motivation of each employee to take control of his or her emotions versus blaming the other person for how they feel. To do this, I suggest you bring each of them into your office individually, and ask them to define the problem. Of course, they will tell you how bad the other person is behaving and may even insist that you do something about it.

At this point, I suggest you partner with their frustration and say something like:

"Wow, I can see how that would be frustrating. I'm curious...on a scale of 1 to 10, how powerful or important do you want (name of the other person) to be in your life?"

They will probably look at you a bit confused, which

is fine, because it has (temporarily, at least) interrupted their righteous indignation. Yous can go on by saying something like:

"It seems as if he (or she) has really gotten under your skin. Do you really want him (or her) to have that kind of power over you?"

Chances are they will respond with some form of, "No!", which is exactly what you want. The good news is that you have now partnered with their reactive brain and used what they are already feeling to open a door that will allow them to change how they react to the other person, to which you could say something like:

"Great! Plus, I think it's fair to say that you might find yourself dealing with other people similar to (name of other person) in the future, right? Therefore, if I could show you a way of working with (name of other person) and others like them in a way that keeps them from getting under your skin, is that something you would want to learn?"

Again, your goal is to open them up to learning how to work with people they would describe as "difficult" so that they can become more productive in this situation and in similar situations in the future.

Of course, if you don't have the time or skill set to coach them on how to keep "difficult" people from getting under their skin, you might want to engage someone like myself who does, because, while you have redefined the problem from the bad behavior of the other person to how that behavior is affecting the employee in your office, this in and of itself won't result in their working together effectively. They will need new skills and a new perspective going forward.

However, because you have opened them up to coaching, and framed this new information in a way that is congruent with what is important to them, the potential that they will hear the coaching as valuable is heightened.

Now, do the same thing with the other employee so that both are working on changing the way they interact with each other and those in your organization.

CHAPTER 10

What to Say...
When You are
Interviewing for a Job

The Problem

Often, when people go for an interview, their highest purpose is to be chosen or hired. While this is understandable, this can trigger the fear of not being hired, which can throw them in to the fear-based, reactive part of the brain. This then can have the interviewee appearing less confident, and even desperate. Further, most interviewers (the people making the decision) have little to no training in interviewing, and just want to find the right person as soon as possible so that they can get back to their real job.

Therefore, they tend to go off their gut feelings, especially if everyone looks good on paper. If they sense awkwardness or a lack of confidence, they tend to think less of the applicant, regardless of their qualifications.

What Not to Say...

I would encourage you not to say things like: "I'm really nervous," or "I know I don't have much experience, but ...," or "I'll do anything for this job." By the same token, you don't want to try to convince the person or persons doing the hiring to hire you. People don't like being convinced.

A Top of the Mind Solution

What you want is to be confident without being cocky, and to give them the impression that you would be someone they would like to work with so that their gut feeling about you is positive. To do this, you need to be clear about your own value, and know that if you were hiring someone for this position, you would hire you.

What to Say...

What they want to know is what you bring to the table that would be a fit for their organization, which means you need to know what their organization is all about. Therefore, in addition to all the things that other career websites tell you to say (You know the company really well. ...You are constantly seeking to learn, ...you want to build a career in the company, etc.) you could also say something like:

"One of the reasons I'm interested in your organization is your focus on accountability (hopefully this is one of their core values, but even if it isn't, it is something every organization wants from its employees). I believe it's my responsibility to bring my best to work every day. I believe it is also my responsibility to be the kind of individual that people enjoy working with."

This gives those who are interviewing you a sense that they aren't going to have to "make you happy" in the position, but that your passion and ability to work with others is something you will be taking responsibility for bringing to the job.

Again, your goal is to project a calm sense of confidence so that they can feel confident in hiring you. To get good at this, I suggest you record some mock interviews, and watch them back to see if you are coming across as someone you would want to hire and work with.

The bottom line is that you need to be clear that if you were the one doing the hiring, you would hire you... and why. This way if they do hire you, that becomes good information about their ability to spot talent. If not, this is also good information about whether you really want the job. In other words, you wouldn't want to work for an organization that doesn't value what you bring to the table, and they have just saved you from having to learn this over a period of time.

CHAPTER 11

What to Say...
When One of Your
Managers Isn't Working
Well with Others.

The Problem

Most people are promoted to the job of manager because they have done their job well. Now, however,
their job is to get other people to do their job well,
and many managers have no idea how to do this
effectively. This can lead to their feeling frustrated, stuck in the brainstem, and blaming everyone
around them.

What Not to Say...

What you don't want to do here is drive them deeper into their brainstem by criticizing their inability to be effective with others.

A Top of the Mind Solution

Instead, you must start where they are, and give them a reason to shift to the upper 80% brain where they can access and improve their people skills.

What to Say...

You could start off by saying something like:

"I notice that some of your people don't seem to be getting what you are wanting them to do."

He or she might then respond with, "Yeah! These are the stupidest people I have ever run across!" or something like that. In other words, they are likely to let you know how they are feeling about their inability to get others to listen to them, to which you could reply with something like:

"Yeah, I can see how that would be frustrating. So, if I could show you how to engage others in such a way that they actually listen and understand what you are wanting them to do, is that something you would like to learn?"

Your goal here isn't to change them into a wonderful, "people person" in one conversation. What you want to do is open them up to coaching. The reason the tactic has the potential to accomplish this goal is that you are partnering with their negative emotions or influencing them by starting with what is already influencing them...their frustration.

Of course, the "coaching" you are wanting them to engage in has to be something that they see as effective. Unfortunately, many managers who are having trouble relating to others tend to see most "people skills" training as psychobabble. Therefore, I suggest that you find a training that is based upon neuropsychology (such as my Life from the Top of the Mind method) versus simple listening skills. When managers can map their effectiveness with others to the part of the brain they are coming from, and the part of the brain they want to engage in those they manage, then the skills of engaging others become something they are more eager to learn.

CHAPTER 12

What to Say...
When You Have Tried
Everything, But Nothing
Works *(The Nuclear Option)*

The Problem

You have tried everything with an employee (training, coaching, giving them chance after chance), and nothing has changed. What you don't want to do is keep doing what isn't working. Not only does this send a negative message to the rest of your organization (you can keep being dysfunctional and you will still be paid), but it also is bad for the problematic employee because it sends them the message that nothing really needs to change.

What Not to Say...

I would encourage you not to say something like: "Come on, (Name), we can't just keep talking about this... something's got to change!" The reason that this is unlikely to be effective is that chances are this isn't the first time you have expressed your frustration, which means the result is likely to be more of the same.

A Top of the Mind Solution

What you want to do is put them in a situation where you aren't trying to "get them to change," but instead get them to commit to either changing or leaving. By the way, this is why I call it "The Nuclear Option." This will blow up the situation one way or the other, which means you must be willing to let this person go if they are not willing to change.

What to Say...

To break this stalemate, I suggest that you bring the problem employee into your office and say something like:

"Okay, (Name), I know we have been going around and around about (whatever you have been trying to get them to do, i.e., get their work in on time, work well with others, etc.) and I'm sure you are as tired of this as I am. So, let's

do this differently.

Let's assume you are interviewing for this job, and I let you know the salary and the benefits, and that based upon your resume, you should be very successful. However, there is one thing that whoever takes this job needs to do, and that is (here you name the thing you have been trying to get them to do, again, for example, get their work in on time, work well with others, engage customers in a professional way, etc.)

So, if this were an interview and you knew that this was a criterion for taking the job... would you take the job?"

Chances are that, for a moment, they won't know what to say because you have asked them a question that requires them to think and make a choice, and purposeful choices come from the neocortex, or "Top of the Mind."

It is important to let them have this time to think, so I suggest you say nothing until they answer either "Yes" or "No."

If they say "No," then you thank them for their candor and give them the gift of unemployment, because what they have just told you is that no matter what you say or do, they have no intention of meeting the requirements of the job.

If they say, "Yes," meaning that they would take the job knowing that (whatever you are trying to get them to do) is a requirement, you say:

"Great! What's going to change?"

Again, you don't say anything until they tell you how they are going to change. You then could say something like:

"Okay, let's create some measurable metrics so that you get credit for the changes you are going to make, and track your progress over the next 4 to 6 weeks. As you know, our organization loves it when people make a commitment to change, and then follow through on that commitment. Of course, you realize that if this isn't something you either want to do, or are able to do, we will have to make some changes. However, I'm confident that if you say you are going to do it, you will!"

This has the potential for calling out the best of who they are, while at the same time, letting them know that if their behavior doesn't change, you will be letting them go.

I call this "The Nuclear Option" because it blows up the experience of trying to get someone to change with little to no results. Also, putting people in an "interview scenario" has them thinking about the future, and the parts of the brain that think about the future are the frontal lobes of the neocortex (what I call the "Top of the Mind").

By the way, while this can be very effective in a business situation, I don't recommend using The Nuclear Option to blow up your friends or family.

CHAPTER 13

What to Say...
When a Customer is
Making Unreasonable
Demands

The Problem

You are being asked to make concessions that you know are not good for your business, and the customer seems to think that the more obnoxious he is, the quicker you will give him what he wants.

What Not to Say...

Unfortunately, simply telling them that they are being unreasonable (or obnoxious) will only have them defend their demanding behavior and make the conversation more contentious.

A Top of the Mind Solution

Instead, I suggest you respond in a way that keeps you in the confident, creative part of the brain, and speaks to the quality of your service or product. The goal here is for you to avoid taking their demands personally and give them a reason to choose to work with you on your terms.

Of course, this assumes that you have set "your terms" with integrity, or in a way that you feel is fair to both you and your customer. If so, your mission here isn't to convince them that their demands are unreasonable (they are unlikely to be convinced), but instead, to given them a chance to become a customer that values doing business with you.

What to Say...

From this perspective, you could say something like:

"I can certainly understand why you would want me to agree with your demands. Unfortunately, I would be doing us both a disservice."

Chances are that they will be a bit confused by this statement, which, when dealing with customers who are making unreasonable demands, isn't such a bad thing. You could then follow it up with something like:

"You see, we take great pride in pricing our services (or products) fairly so that it serves all parties. We hire quality people who take a lot of responsibility for what they do. This can cost a bit more, but the payoff is in the quality of their work. We both know that there are other companies that would just tell you what you wanted to hear and find a way to make it work for them by cutting corners. We aren't that kind of company.

Therefore, if you feel our price is unreasonable, or you have decided that we aren't the type of organization you want to work with, then I think it would be to both of our benefits for you to take your business elsewhere. However, if you would like to work with us now and in the future and want to continue discussing how we might accommodate your budget without cutting corners, then I suggest we keep talking. What works for you?"

Assuming that what you have told your customer is true (i.e., you have priced your products or services in a way that is good for both your employees and your customers), then you really only want to create relationships with customers who appreciate you (and, therefore, will purchase from you again and recommend you to their friends). Many businesses say that they spend 80% of their time trying to please 20% of their problem customers. I suggest you not follow their lead.

CHAPTER 14

What to Say...
When You Want A Raise

The Problem

Most people go into the experience of asking for a raise thinking that they have to convince "the powers that be" that they deserve to be paid more for what they do. This automatically puts leadership in a position between what you feel is best for you and what they feel is best for them and/or the organization.

What Not to Say

Therefore, you don't want to go in to the meeting listing all of the reasons you should get a raise that have to do with you (i.e., you have been there for so many years, you do the work of two people, you really need the money, etc.).

A Top of the Mind Solution

What you want to do is frame your rationale for a raise in terms of what is good for the leadership and / or the organization. In other words, how is giving you a raise going to benefit them?

What to Say...

"First, I appreciate your openness to discussing my salary. I know that attracting and retaining the best and the brightest is important for the success of this organization. I also know that my worth to the organization is dependent on my contributions. I do not believe that you want people who just show up and do the minimum. Therefore, I would be happy to outline how my commitment to going above and beyond has benefited the organization." (Here, you speak to your contributions and try to tie a dollar amount to each, either in terms of the income you have generated or the money you have saved the organization).

You finish with:

"Given all of this, I feel that your increased investment in me and my skills will continue to pay dividends, and I look forward to demonstrating my value to the organization with the kind of hard work and dedication to excellence

that you expect and that I bring to my job every day."

Of course, they may have some pushback on your request, citing the difficult economy, competition from other organizations, limited resources, etc., to which you could say something like:

"Yes, I understand that you must always keep in mind what is good for the organization in making your decision. And, if I didn't think that my increased salary would result in increased productivity and profits, I wouldn't be asking for a raise. All I ask is that you take my previous efforts on your behalf, as well as your desire to attract and retain the best and the brightest into account when determining my compensation."

Here, you have done about all you can do to make your case. If they still don't want to give you the raise you feel you deserve, it may be time to look around to see if there are other organizations that do see your value.

Section III
Friends & Family

CHAPTER 15

What to Say... When Your Friends Keep Coming to You With their Troubles

The Problem

You have a friend (or friends) who continually come to you with stories about all the negative things that are happening in their lives, and/or all the bad feelings they have about themselves and the world. You want to be supportive, but it's wearing you down because you don't know how to fix their problems, and you are not even sure that they are truly looking for solutions.

What Not to Say

In these situations, just sympathizing, or trying to

give your friends ideas about how to feel better rarely produces results. Therefore, I would encourage you not to say something like, "Gosh, I'm so sorry, that must be awful." Or, "Well, have you tried (all the solutions you have tried to give them in the past)." While empathizing with them does show that you care, and can be helpful for those grieving a loss, for constant complainers, it just tends to validate how bad their life is. If people are just looking for a sympathetic ear, this will not motivate them to change.

In fact, there is something in psychology called "secondary gains," which speaks to the fact that some people really like the attention and sympathy they receive when they share their troubles with others. And, of course, given how many times you have tried to offer solutions only to have them either ignored or rejected outright, you know that this isn't the way to go.

A Top of the Mind Solution

What you want is to be able to show you care without feeding their depression, worries, or fears, and to motivate them to change, if possible.

What to Say...

Therefore, I suggest you say something like:

"Wow, I can see how you would feel badly about that, and I wish I had the skills to help you. Unfortunately, I don't know how to solve your problems. However, there are people out there who do have the skills to help people change their lives, and I have every confidence that when it gets bad enough, you will reach out for help. I'm sure that's what you would recommend to someone you love."

There is a quote that says, "Some people will never change until the misery of the present becomes worse than the mystery of the future." In other words, if you do succeed in helping someone feel better, that may actually diminish their motivation to get professional help because the problem is no longer as painful.

However, when you respond in a way similar to my suggestion, you not only show that you care, you point them in the direction that they need to go (i.e., getting help from a professional), and express confidence that, sooner or later, they will have the courage to get the help they need. Plus, you let them know that this is how you are going to respond to them in the future, which means that they may stop coming to you if sympathy is all they are looking for.

CHAPTER 16

What to Say...
When Your Toddler is
Throwing a Tantrum

The Problem

Your toddler is in "meltdown mode," and nothing you do seems to work. If this is out in public, you may be embarrassed, which only adds to your frustration.

What Not to Say...

What you don't want to do is try to reason with your children when this is happening, because they are stuck in the "unreasonable" brain (the brainstem). All they know is that they are frustrated beyond belief, and every time they are told to stop, this only frustrates them even more. Therefore, I would not encourage you to fall back on the old parental stand-by, "If you don't stop crying I will give you something to cry about!" Nor would I encourage you to use your superior physical strength to try to "make them" stop. To be clear, I also wouldn't encourage you to give into what they are crying about, because that teaches them to go into hysterics whenever they don't get what they want.

A Top of the Mind Solution

What you want is to motivate them to stop crying without needing to reason with them or threaten them. You then want to address the tendency to throw a tantrum so that this happens less in the future.

What to Say...

The key here is to take away the power of the tantrum to frustrate you into giving in, and introduce something into the conversation that interrupts the cycle of anger and frustration that is so characteristic of meltdowns. To do this, I suggest trying something that psychology calls, "prescribing the symptom." This might sound something like:

"Wow! That is the best tantrum I have ever seen! Do you think you can keep this up for about an hour?

Of course, the child is set on disagreeing with what-ever you suggest, and, therefore, is likely to respond with a somewhat confused, but determined, "No!," to which you can say,

Are you sure?

...in which he or she will repeat, "No!" You can then say:

"Okay, if you say so."

Because the cycle of frustration has been interrupted and the power of the tantrum to embarrass you is no longer a factor, your child will probably start to wind down. It's important to give him or her space to do this so that they don't start to see you as someone who is trying to "calm them down."

Of course, this will only work one or two times, and, therefore, I suggest you become more proactive in dealing with your child's negative emotions in the future. The way to do this is to tap into your child's natural desire to have fun. I call this desire to feel good or have fun their "highest purpose," and the good news is that this is common to almost all chil-dren. They wake up in the morning asking, "How can I have fun?" and often get frustrated when we get in the way of this goal. Again, the good news is that you can partner with this desire to help them learn to handle their frustrations and cut down on tantrums in the future.

The key is to catch them right after they have been having fun and get them to reflect on this experience. You could say something like:

"Wow, I noticed you were really having a good time"

Your child will very likely agree with you and start telling you about what they were doing. After listening, you could then say something like:

"Yeah! And yet, I remember the other day when we were upset about (whatever the last upset was all about), that wasn't much fun, was it?"

By the way, notice that I used the word "we" versus "you." You don't want to have your child thinking that you are blaming them for the upsetting situation. Your child is likely to agree with you that this wasn't much fun. You could then say something like:

"Yeah, I like having fun and feeling good versus feeling bad, don't you?"

You will most likely get more agreement, which is what you want. Plus, you have added "feeling good" to "having fun" which will be important going forward. You could then say something like:

"So, if we could find a way to feel good and have more fun in the future versus feeling bad, would that be a good idea?"

More agreement. So, you could say:

"Okay, what if we had a magic word we could use whenever one of us starts to feel bad, and when we hear that word, we will change from feeling bad to feeling good… would that be cool?"

Kids love magic and games, and, therefore, your child will probably be all in for this. You could say:

"Great! What should our magic word be?"

It's best to let them come up with the word to ensure that it is meaningful to them. Let's say they like "bananas." You could say:

"Great, so the next time I start to get mad or frustrated, you can say "bananas," and I will stop and take a deep breath and do something silly so that I feel good, okay? Let's practice. I will start to get mad and you say the magic word."

It's important that you model what you want your child to do first so that they have some sense of what this would look like, and, of course, we can never ask our kids to do something we aren't willing to do. You might want to take a few deep breaths when you hear the magic word because this is what you want your child to do when they begin to get frustrated. After you have responded to the magic word, you say:

"Great! Now you start to get mad or frustrated, and I will say the magic word."

Chances are this will go very well, so be sure to praise and compliment your child for doing so well. In fact, you might want to set up a "star chart" so that you and your child get a star every time either one of you is able to shift from "mad" to "glad" (with your child being able to turn his or her stars into a toy after accumulating a certain number).

The overall goal here is to use your children's love of fun and feeling good to help them deal with feeling bad, and teaching them a process to interrupt the escalation of frustration. To make this even more powerful, you can teach your children to talk to you about what they are wanting or are frustrated about, before going into meltdown mode.

.

CHAPTER 17

What to Say...
When Your Parents Aren't
Supporting Your Dreams

The Problem

Your parents believe that the degree or career you are pursuing won't result in your being able to make a good living. Chances are they are pushing you toward more traditional careers that pay well. Unfortunately, you may need their financial support to finish college, and, of course, you would love their emotional support as well.

What Not to Say...

If you haven't noticed, arguing with your parents only results in their becoming more determined to convince you that they are right. Therefore, I would not encourage you to say something like, "You just don't understand! " or, "It's my life! Why don't you let me live it!" While your frustration is understandable, it will only drive you deeper into the reactive brain, and have your parents seeing you as someone who doesn't listen to reason (which becomes one more reason for them to make this decision for you).

A Top of the Mind Solution

Therefore, what you want to do is engage your parents in a way that has them seeing you as the intelligent, accomplished, and thoughtful young adult you are, which has the potential to result in their supporting your decision, even if they disagree. You also want to frame going forward in a way that allows their love for you and your love for them to be part of the process.

What to Say…

"Mom and Dad, I know you love me and want the best for me, and that your idea of what I should pursue as a career is driven by that love and support. That means a lot to me and I never want to take that for granted.

I also can see that how we have talked about this in the past has been less than successful, and I feel I should start by taking more responsibility for how I am with you.

In other words, would it be fair to say that, in the past, you don't feel as if I have truly heard and understood what you were trying to tell me?"

Here, they are likely to agree with this, to which you can respond with something like:

"That makes sense, and I can see how frustrating that was, given your desire to help. So, let's change that. If I work hard at truly listening and understanding your position, would you be willing to do the same for me?"

Here they might say, "Well, of course, this is what we have been doing all along." I encourage you not to get into a debate about whether this is true or not, but to just let that go right by you and say something like:

"Great, so help me understand what's important to you here… what do you want me to know about this situation?"

Here you want to give your parents every opportunity to state their concerns, otherwise they are going to think you haven't really heard them, which could lead to their rejecting your perspective. Try not to take their concerns as an indication of their lack of faith in you. They probably just want the best for you.

Once they have finished, I would say something like:

"That makes sense, I can see where you are coming from. Do you feel I have done a better job of listening and working to understand you?"

They should say, yes, to this because you have, and you can then ask,

"Thanks! Would you be willing to do the same for me?"

Again, even if they say, "Well, of course, this is what we always do," don't get into an argument about whether this is true. Just say "wonderful," and lay out your perspective in a way that has the highest potential for them to support you (See below). However, if they still need to tell you all the reasons why you shouldn't pursue this career, it will be important to listen versus get back into an argument about who is right.

Once they have said everything they need to say, I suggest you say something like:

"Again, that makes sense. I know you love me and only have my happiness and well-being in mind. So, let me lay out my reasoning

To be clear, I'm aware that what I love to do does not guarantee a good job at a good salary upon graduation. I'm

*under no illusions here. However, what it will do is give
me a sense of what it is like to do what I love for a living.
And, I feel this could be priceless. So, let's say this could
go two ways, one, I could graduate, become very successful
and wind up buying both of you your dream home. Or, it
is certainly possible that I will graduate and after giving
it my best shot, decide that I want to find work that pays
me a decent salary.*

*Even in this worst-case scenario, I will have spent four
years loving every day, and I will be able to take this experience into the choice of a new career. Basically, it means
I will never wind up hating my job like so many people
do. Plus, I will have a bachelor's degree, and, therefore,
can apply for any job that requires a college degree. And,
most importantly, your willingness to support my degree
will mean the world to me, which means rather than this
continuing to be something we argue about, this will be an
opportunity for me to take responsibility for the grades I
make, and for supporting myself once I graduate…No asking you to subsidize my choice of career post-graduation.*

*Mom, Dad, I know you might make a different choice here,
and, it would mean so much to me if you could support
me in following my dream. It may or may not come true,
but, regardless, I will have given it my best shot, put my
all into college, learned to do what I love for a living, and,
therefore, will never live a life wondering "what if." Is
this something you are willing to do?"*

Okay, I get that this is VERY long, and you would probably say it differently. However, I'm not suggesting that you memorize this and say it verbatim (unless, of course, you can do that in a way that is natural for you). What I really want you to get here are the concepts of listening to understand another's perspective, acknowledging that this makes sense to them, using love as a foundation for discussing differences of opinion, and asking for support rather than agreement.

Plus, in the text above, I have introduced some concepts that your parents may not have thought of... specifically, the idea that supporting your dream will have you taking more responsibility for your grades in college and that this experience will serve you, regardless of whether you become successful in your chosen career (because it has taught you the value of doing what you love).

Some people like to write this in a letter (and I do suggest a handwritten letter versus a text or email) so that your parents can read it and think about it without having to respond right away. The bottom line is that you want to have your parents support you in your decision, even though they may not think it is the best for you. This will be tough for them, however, if they see that you have thought this through and are willing to take responsibility for your success post college (and that their support will help you feel closer to them during the process), they may be willing to put their concerns aside, and support you in following your dream.

By the way, if you want to know how to deal with the stress, anxiety, and lack of certainty that can come with a degree in the Arts, feel free to check out my book, "Freeing The Artistic Mind." (You can read reviews from students and faculty in the performing arts at https://www.billcrawfordphd.com/performing-arts.)

CHAPTER 18

What to Say...
When Your Ex Is Being
A Jerk!

The Problem

You are divorced, but still are co-parents to your child or children. However, the animosity that reared its ugly head during the divorce is getting in the way of cooperation when it comes to your kids. In fact, it seems as if your ex is just being difficult out of spite.

What Not to Say...

What you don't want to do is become frustrated and point out how your ex is being uncooperative or accuse him or her of being spiteful. This will just have them defending the behavior you want them to change.

A Top of the Mind Solution

Instead, I suggest that you frame your communication in terms of something you both agree upon, which (hopefully) is the love each of you have for your children.

What to Say…

Therefore, I suggest you say something like:

"I know that we both have a lot of hurt feelings from the divorce. And, I also know we love (name(s) of your child/children) more than we are angry with each other. Therefore, going forward, I am willing to cooperate with you in a way that if (name(s) of your child/children) were watching, he (or she, or they) would be proud of their mom and dad. Will you join me?"

Of course, this doesn't mean that everything will be rosy and wonderful, but what you will have done is introduce a reason for your ex to cooperate with you that has more to do with love versus animosity. And, if you can keep this love for your children as the energy between you and your ex, then that will only bode well for communication going forward.

CHAPTER 19

What to Say...
When Your Parents are Still
Treating You Like a Child

The Problem

Your parents seem to be relishing the role of decision-makers and advisors, which unfortunately puts you in the position of someone who isn't able to make your own decisions, and/or follow your own advice.

What Not to Say...

Telling your parents that they need to stop treating you like a child only makes you sound childish, which validates their belief that you can't make good decisions on your own. Plus, in general, criticizing someone's behavior only has them defending the very behavior you want them to change. Chances are that being your parent may be one of the most important roles they feel they have, which makes them reluctant to give it up.

Plus, they may be concerned that if you don't need them, they will fade from your life, which has the potential to leave them feeling useless or abandoned.

A Top of the Mind Solution

What you want to do is frame your request in a way that matches your love for them and their love for you, as well as what's important to them, and what's important to you.

What to Say...

Therefore, you could say something like:

"Mom, Dad, I want to thank you for always being there for me and looking out for me. I know that comes from your love, and I will be forever grateful for that. And, I'm sure we all know that for me to be successful, I have to learn to stand on my own two feet and learn from my mistakes, just like you did. Therefore, it would mean so much to me if you could show me how much you love me by trusting me to make my own decisions and only giving me your advice when I ask for it. Would you be

willing to do that?

The reason this has the potential to be effective is that you aren't trying to get them to change by criticizing their desire to parent you. Plus, you never mentioned the words "treat me like a child." Instead, you are partnering with the desire of every parent, which is for their children to learn to stand on their own two feet and become a responsible adult.

Of course, this doesn't mean that they will never treat you like a child again. However, it does give you a way of addressing any future slip-ups on their part in such a way that taps into their love and parental desire to have you become a successful adult, versus their need to stay involved in your life by continuing to tell you what to do.

By the way, showing them how respecting you and treating you like an adult can actually result in your feeling closer to them will help this process along.

CHAPTER 20

What to Say...
When Someone Is Trying To
Make You Feel Guilty

The Problem

A member of your family (or your relationship partner) is trying to "guilt trip" you into doing or not
doing something.

What Not to Say...

What you don't want to do is confront them and
accuse them of trying to make you feel guilty. The
potential that they will agree with you, apologize,
and never do it again is slim to none. Instead, they
are likely to defend their original statement.

A Top of the Mind Solution

What you want, instead, is to communicate that you are not going to be manipulated by their attempt to make you feel guilty, but to do this in such a way that they change their behavior without taking offense at what you say.

What To Say...

In this case, I suggest you say something like:

"Yes, I can understand why you would want me to (do or not do whatever). However, I have noticed that when I agree to something that really doesn't work for me, I start to feel resentful. Therefore, in order to avoid bringing resentment into our family (or relationship), I'm going to trust my instincts in this situation. Thanks for understanding."

Of course, they will probably not understand, but that is not necessarily your goal here (i.e., convincing them to stop trying to use guilt to manipulate you). Instead, your goal is to set a healthy boundary where you are making the decisions about what you do or don't do in a way that they will have difficulty rebutting. This doesn't mean that they won't try. However, you can always just smile and say:

"Yes, I can see how you would see it that way... and...

this is my decision."

Once you say that a few times, they will come to understand that you aren't going to argue with them (which means they can't attack your argument), and they will probably give up and go try to "guilt trip" someone else.

CHAPTER 21

What to Say...
When Your Aging Parents
Won't Listen to
Your Advice

The Problem

Your parents are at the point in their lives where they need your assistance in certain matters, such as, long-term care, transportation (they may still insist on driving), medication, healthcare, finances, etc. Unfortunately, they are used to giving advice versus taking it, and are often resistant, and even resentful, when you try to help.

What Not to Say...

Trying to convince them that they need you, or that they are no longer capable of making these decisions

rarely works because it taps into their greatest fear…
losing control. Sadly, they are seeing their friends
pass away, and are frightened by the fact that they
can do less and less as they grow older and older,
which has them seeing your desire to help as a threat
to their independence.

A Top of the Mind Solution

What you want to do is engage them in a way that
has them seeing you as someone they love (and
who loves them) and respects their desire to be as
independent as possible for as long as possible. Plus,
if there are grandchildren involved, tap into their
(and your) love for their grandchildren as a way to
establish some common ground using love versus
fear as the energy for communication.

What to Say…

If there has been conflict in the past about their
resistance to taking your advice, you must address
this first. In this case, you could say something like:

*"Mom, Dad, I want you to know that I love you more than
life itself, and, I'm guessing that there may have been times
in the past when you haven't felt loved and respected by
me, especially when we have argued. Fair to say?"*

I'm pretty sure, that they will agree to this. If so, you

could say something like:

"First, I apologize for this. I think my concern about your well-being had me getting frustrated, and that must have felt anything but loving. Therefore, I plan on changing this. From now on, I am going to take 100% responsibility for engaging you in a way that you feel loved and respected, and I know you will do the same with me.

In fact, if I were talking to you in the future about long-term care issues, and other matters regarding your well-being in a way that you felt loved and respected, what would that look like from your end? How would I be acting or reacting differently than I have in the past?"

This will be important information because it will tell you how you can best get your ideas across, while at the same time, giving your parents an opportunity to have some say-so or control over the process.

To which you can reply:

"Great! I will try to do that, and if for some reason you feel that I'm not treating you with love and respect, will you let me know?"

I know this may sound dangerous to some, because it might bring up fears of you being criticized at every turn. However, remember, our goal is to know when we are being perceived as controlling or unloving so that we can change (and, as a result, be more effective in the interaction). Plus, remember, also, that they are frightened and are losing control of many aspects of their lives. Therefore, as someone who loves them, and someone who isn't losing control of your life the way they are, you must be the bigger person here if you want to be successful.

Next, we want to step away from the power struggle and use love versus fear as a way to address decisions. As discussed in the introduction, fear (their fear of losing control and of dying, and your fear that they aren't making rational decisions) will throw all parties into the brainstem, or the resistant part of the brain. This is what has triggered the conflict... resentment, resistance, and arguments in the past, and will continue to do so unless you change the energy that is driving the interactions.

The good news is that you have already laid a foundation for this change by the new way you have approached them, and that may be enough to change the tone of future conversations. However, if you wanted to go one step further along the path of bringing love into the picture as the energy that will drive future discussions, you might say something like:

"How about this? I know how much you love (names of their grandchildren/your children) and I know how im-

portant it is that we are role models for them. Therefore, how about we commit to discussing things in the future in a way we would want (names of their grandchildren/ your children) to copy... as if they were watching and taking notes, and we wanted them to emulate what they saw... could we try this?"

It's hard to imagine that they will disagree with this suggestion, and, therefore, you will have created one more reason for discussions in the future to be more productive and less confrontational. Plus, if you do find yourself getting frustrated (or if any future interactions become contentious), you can use this as a way to stop the discussion so that everyone can cool off. You could say something like:

"You know, I don't feel like I'm interacting with you at the moment in a way I would like (names of their grandchildren/your children) to emulate. Therefore, I'm going to take a few minutes (or longer, if necessary) to calm down. How about we talk about this again later?"

There is a quote I love that says: "The first rule of holes: When you are in one, stop digging!" This means that what you don't want to do is continue the sort of problematic discussions you have had in the past, thus, tapping into everyone's love for the children in your family will be a great way to keep this from happening.

Chapter 22

What to Say...
When You Want to Heal a
Relationship with
Friends or Family

The Problem

Something has happened in the past that has caused a riff between you and a friend or family member. Because of the hurt feelings and/or anger and resentment this has caused, interactions have been strained or nonexistent ever since.

What Not to Say...

Generally, suggesting that everyone "let bygones be bygones," or "let's forget the past and move on" doesn't work. Often, each person feels that they were wronged, and that their negative feelings are valid.

A Top of the Mind Solution

If this relationship is truly important to you, you must be willing to start by owning your part of any past issue. Then, you must frame the solution in a way that taps into the good feelings you shared with this person in the past and lay a foundation for getting this back to going forward.

What to Say...

Given this, you could say something like:

"(Name of person) I've been thinking about the problems we had in the past, and I'm saddened because I remember how close we were at one time. I would like to see if we could be close again, and if that is something you would like as well. Of course, we can't just pretend that nothing happened, and so, I'm willing to take responsibility for my part. In fact, thinking back, I have an idea of what I would do differently. Would you be open to hearing what I have learned?"

The goal here is to open up a conversation about how things can be different between you two in the future. However, that must include some acknowledgment of what happened, and what you would do differently if something like this happens again. This could include a willingness to listen to the other person's point of view before forming a conclusion, or keeping the value of the relationship in mind as you dealt with the problem, or working to see how a misunderstanding might have had you coming across in a way that seemed critical, etc.

This is what you want them to do with you, right? If so, you must be willing to model the behavior you want to inspire. One way of thinking about this is imagining your children (or someone who looks up to you) coming to you and asking how to repair a relationship that is important to them but has been damaged by some past interaction.

Of course, if the incident that caused the split was your "fault" (meaning you made some significant mistake), then apologizing will be an important first step. You could say something like:

"First I want to apologize for the choices I made in the past that harmed our relationship. I recognize that my actions have caused you to question whether you can trust me. I want you to know that your trust is important to me, and that I understand it will take some time to earn that back. I'm sure you will need to see evidence that I have learned from my mistake, and I'm willing to take 100% responsibility for being the sort of person you can trust going forward. I hope that what we had in the past is worth giving the relationship another shot."

Again, your goal here is to own your part of the problem, and let the other person know how much you value the relationship. Of course, it's possible that no matter what you do or say, they may be unwilling to give the relationship another try or accept your apology. If that is the case, it will be unfortunate, however, something that you will want to work on accepting.

The truth is that they have a right to decide who they create (or recreate) relationships with, and if that is their decision, there is really nothing you can do about it. Plus, you wouldn't want to be in a relationship with someone that you had to convince to like you anyway. Therefore, if this is the case, I suggest you move on, taking what you have learned, and applying it to new relationships in the future.

CHAPTER 23

What to Say...
When You Want to Stop
Becoming Frustrated at
Family Gatherings

The Problem

You have found yourself becoming angry, defensive, or reverting to feeling like a child at family gatherings. This can be especially problematic because you don't want to divorce your family, however, you also don't want this to continue.

What Not to Say...

You have probably tried telling your family to stop treating you this way with little to no results. In fact, most people take such criticism personally, and actually start defending the behavior you want them to change. Therefore, I would not encourage you to point out their negative behavior or what you want them to change.

A Top of the Mind Solution

This is a problem that has come up a lot in my counseling with individuals, and, therefore, I have created what I call a "Family Letter" that is sent to your family before the holiday or event such as a family reunion. The goal of the letter is to address the problem in a way that doesn't accuse them, but does lay a foundation for behavior change.

What to Say...

Here is a sample version of this letter:

"Dear _____ ,

I just wanted to drop you a note and give you a heads-up on something I am working on with respect to the qualities and characteristics I bring to my interactions with people, and especially those I am close to, such as you. You see, in looking back at some of my interactions in the past, I don't feel I have been as purposeful as I would like. Therefore, I have made a decision that from now on, I will take 100% responsibility for the qualities and characteristics that I bring to all of my interactions, which means I will choose those qualities that we would want to teach to (names of

your children or grandchildren, nieces, nephews, etc.).
I'm sure you would agree that given we are role models
for (names of your children) we always want to interact
with each other in a way we would want them to emulate.

Therefore, in the future, if I find myself unable to access the
qualities of love, respect, and caring that I want to teach to
_____, or if I feel that we are interacting with each other in
a way that we would not want (names of your children) to
emulate, I will excuse myself until I'm able to once again
be the role model I want to be. Just know that this is not
meant as criticism. It's just me taking responsibility for
the quality of my interactions and what I am teaching
(names of your children). Thanks for understanding.

Love (you)

Again, the purpose of this letter is to let them know
that something is going to change without making
them defensive by criticizing their behavior. I do
encourage this to be sent in the form of a letter for
several reasons. 1) No one gets letters anymore,
and that will make this special. 2) It will give those
members of your family time to read it over (probably several times) without having to respond at
that moment.

Of course, it is possible that your family will think
you have lost your mind and be very confused by
this. I don't see this as a problem, because you are

just describing how you are going to respond differently in the future, and you are using what you want to teach your children (their grandchildren, nieces, nephews, etc.) as a criteria for change. That is hard to argue with.

However, let's say that they do come back with: "What's this weird letter all about?" You could say something like:

"Oh, no big deal, I just wanted you to know how I'm taking more responsibility for the qualities and characteristics that I bring to my relationships going forward, so that if I do need to excuse myself to ensure I'm responding to those I love in a way I would want the children in our family to emulate, you will know what's going on."

Of course, it will be important that you follow through on your commitment to only engage others when the conversation is something you would want your children to copy. However, if you are willing to stick to the criteria, it will alter the dynamics in your family in a way that you control and without you needing to criticize anyone in order to create this change.

CHAPTER 24

What to Say...
When You Want
Your Kids to Go to Bed

The Problem

This is something almost all parents struggle with, because to kids, going to bed means they have to stop having fun, and given that "having fun" is their highest purpose, they resist this.

What Not to Say...

Even though we can "make them" do what we want through anger or physical force, I would encourage you to avoid this method of influence. Why? Well, not only do our kids feel badly when yelled at, we, as parents, feel badly as well. This is not what we want the energy to be between us and our children whom we love more than life itself. Therefore, phrases, such as, "I'm getting angry!" or, "I'm going to count to three, and if you don't..." are not only no fun for us, they actually teach our kids not to pay any attention to us until we get angry.

A Top of the Mind Solution

The key here is to have them get the sleep they need, while at the same time, teaching them a quality that you want them to have when they become adults. The truth is that every time we interact with our kids, we are teaching them something, and because we aren't really raising "kids" any more than a chicken farmer is raising chicks, we need to ensure that we aren't just "making them go to bed," but instead teaching them to make and keep agreements.

This starts by giving them choices, because we make purposeful choices from the upper 80% of the brain (or the Top of the Mind). Of course, this doesn't mean that we let them choose not to go to bed, because that would be bad for their health.

What to Say...

I suggest that you pop your head into the room where they are playing about fifteen minutes before you would like them to start getting ready for bed, and say something like:

"Hey kids, would you like to go to bed now or play for 15 minutes?"

Of course, they are almost certain to say, "Play for 15 minutes!"

To which you could respond with:

"Okay, I'm going to set a buzzer for 15 minutes (you always want to have a buzzer or alarm so it's not you stopping their play) and when it goes off, what will you do?"

They will probably say, "Put on our pajamas, bush our teeth" or whatever they normally do as a bedtime routine.

You say, *"Great!"* and set the buzzer. *Then, because kids don't really have a good concept of time, I suggest that you stick your head in at about five minutes and say, "Five Minutes!" ...then again at one minute and say, "One Minute!"*

I can't tell you how many parents have told me that when the buzzer goes off, their kids get up and go do what they have agreed to do. If this happens, you really want to praise them and tell them how proud you are of them, because this reinforces this same behavior in the future.

Of course, it's possible that, given how much they love to have fun, they might say, "We want to play some more." If this happens, you can say something like:

"Oh, well, we had an agreement, you know, and, I'm curious, when I agree to take you to (their favorite place, the zoo, the park etc.), is that an agreement that you want me to keep?"

They will very likely say, "Yes" to this, to which you can respond with:

"Oh, so you want to live in a house where everyone keeps their agreements, right? So, if we can keep our agreements, I can let you play for an extra fifteen minutes every night. If not, we may have to start going to bed really early, like around 5:30, and I know you don't want that, right?"

The reason all of this has the potential to be effective is that you are doing several things, 1) You are giving them choices, which puts them in the part of the brain that makes purposeful choices (the neocortex), and 2) You are teaching them to make and keep agreements... a quality or characteristic you want them to have when they become adults, and 3) You are tapping into what is important to them (having fun) to drive their willingness to cooperate.

All of this means that you are engaging their receptive brain versus their resistant brain, which means that they are more likely to want to cooperate. Plus, you are coming from the purposeful part of your brain (versus your frustration, anger, or exasperation) when getting them to do what you want.

A lot of what you are going to hear in this section on parenting has to do with the concept of purposefulness and recognizing that anytime we are interacting with our kids, we are teaching them something, and what we want to teach are qualities we want them to have when they become adults. This means we can't teach respect by being disrespectful. We can't teach cooperation by being uncooperative. We can't instill confidence by interacting with them in a way that implies that we have no confidence in them.

Therefore, whether we are putting them to bed or helping them pick out their first car, we always want to keep in mind that they are learning from us ALL OF THE TIME, which, of course, is what we want (meaning we want to be good role models for our kids).

CHAPTER 25

What to Say...
When Your Child Seems to
Be Anxious About
Everything

The Problem

Nature seems to have "blessed" you with what some call "an anxious child" who seems to be afraid and/or worried in ways that you consider to be abnormal. This can cause problems with schedules (you're trying to get out the door, and he or she is melting down about one thing or another) and, at times can even become a drag on the entire family.

What Not to Say...

What most people try to do is convince their child that there isn't anything to be anxious about. Unfortunately, this often has the child defending the validity of his or her anxiety and becoming more anxious. Other parents try to bribe their child to stop crying or whining, and that can backfire as well, because it teaches the child that anxiety gets them attention and/or what they want. Unfortunately, when they are feeling anxious, they are stuck in their "anxious brain," or the "resistant brain" (the brainstem), and no amount of reason or cajoling is likely to get them to change. Of course, you do want to help them, but trying to do this while they are in "melt-down mode" is rarely effective.

A Top of the Mind Solution

Instead, I suggest that you tap into the fact that kids don't like feeling bad, and in fact, as mentioned earlier, their mission on the planet is to have fun. Therefore, the key is to catch them right after they have been having fun so that they are in their "receptive, cooperative brain."

What to Say…

The goal is to get them to actually feel the difference between "feeling good" and "feeling bad," and then show them how to influence more of how they want to feel and less of how they don't. The good news is that we have already learned how to do this earlier in Chapter 16 when we learned how to stop kids from throwing tantrums. Therefore, I'm going to revisit what we learned and apply it to general anxiety. So, you could say something like:

"Hey, I noticed that you were having a great time just now. That must have felt really good!"

Your child will very likely agree with you and start telling you what was so enjoyable about what they were doing. After listening, you could then say something like:

"Yeah! And yet, I remember the other day when we were upset about (whatever the last upset was all about), that wasn't much fun, was it?"

By the way, notice I used the word "we" versus "you." You don't want to have your child thinking that you are blaming them for their being anxious. Your child is likely to agree with you that this wasn't much fun. You could then say something like:

"Yeah, I like having fun and feeling good versus feeling bad, don't you?"

You will most likely get more agreement, which is what you want. Plus, you have added "feeling good" to "having fun," which will be important going forward. You could then say something like:

"So, if we could find a way to have fun, feel good, and have more fun in the future versus feeling bad, would that be a good idea?"

More agreement. So, you could then say:

"Okay, what if we had a magic word we could use whenever one of us starts to feel bad, and when we hear that word, we can change from feeling bad to feeling good... would that be nice?"

Kids love magic and games, and therefore, your child will probably be all in for this. You could say:

"Great, what should our magic word be?"

Best to let them come up with the word to ensure that it is meaningful to them. Let's say they like "bananas." You could say:

"Great, so the next time I start to get anxious, you can say "bananas," and I will stop and take a deep breath and do something silly so that I feel good, okay? Let's practice. I will start to get anxious and you say the magic word."

It's important that you model what you want your child to do first so that they have some sense of what this would look like, and, of course, we can never ask our kids to do something we aren't willing to do. You might want to take a few deep breaths when you hear the magic word because this is what you want your child to do when they begin to get frustrated. After you have responded to the magic word, you say:

"Great, now you start to get anxious and I will say the magic word."

Chances are that this will go very well, so be sure to praise and compliment your child for doing so well. In fact, you might want to set up a "star chart" so that you and your child gets a star every time either one of you is able to shift from anxious to glad (with your child being able to turn his or her stars into the purchase of a toy after accumulating a certain number).

The overall goal here is to use your children's love of fun and feeling good to help them deal with feeling bad, and teaching them a process to interrupt the escalation of anxiety. To make this even more powerful, you can teach your children to talk to you about what they are wanting or are anxious about before going into meltdown mode.

It is important to note that seeing the world in an anxious way has probably become a habit with your child, and, therefore, don't expect this to change overnight. Plus, you don't want your child to become ashamed of his or her emotions. The key is to give them a way to influence how they feel so that they can learn to manage their anxiety early in life. This possibly could prevent them from becoming an anxious teen or adult in the future as well.

In my book, "Life from the Top of the Mind," I teach readers a model for shifting from the lower, anxious brain to the upper, clear, confident, and cooperative brain. The model uses principals of mindfulness and imagery to accomplish this switch, and I have been told that kids love it.

CHAPTER 26

What to Say...
When Your Teenager Seems
to Ignore You, or Won't
Cooperate with You

The Problem

You try to engage your teenager, but they treat you as if you are annoying them. This can be problematic, not only because it leaves you feeling unloved and disrespected, but because it shuts down communication between you and those you love, and for whom you are responsible.

What Not to Say…

It's important not to let your annoyance at being ignored drive your attempt to solve the problem. In other words, you don't want to say something like,

"Hello!!!!!! I'm trying to talk to you here! Could you at least pretend to pay attention!"

This reminds me of a concept that I teach in my seminars called "The You Stupid Idiot" rule. Basically, I suggest that we never talk to someone in a way where they could put "you stupid idiot" on the end of anything we say. It encourages those of us who want to become more influential with others to ensure that we aren't angry, frustrated, or annoyed when trying to talk to them, because this will leak into our tone of voice, and they will hear us calling them a stupid idiot whether we mean to or not. This will drive them deeper into their resistant brain and have them rejecting anything we say.

Therefore, if we want to be influential with our teenagers, we must not allow our anger or frustration to color our communications.

A Top of the Mind Solution

First, we need to recognize that our teenagers may not be trying to frustrate us, ignore us, or imply that they don't love and respect us. They are in the time of their lives where their developmental task is to figure out who they are separate from us. This means that, while we have been VERY important in their lives as children, in order for them to eventually become independent, they need to first be "not us." The key, therefore, is not to take their behavior personally or interpret it to mean that they no longer love us. To be clear, this doesn't mean we just put up with it. We just want to approach the issue in a way that has the potential to be successful, and in a way that strengthens our relationship with our teenager.

It is wise here to approach our teenager at a time where there is no conflict going on, and in a way that taps into what is important to them. In general, for a teenager, this is with independence and respect. In other words, when they feel that we are limiting their independence or treating them "like a child," as they might phrase it, they will become resistant.

What to Say...

You might start with something that you feel confident that they will respond to positively. This might sound something like:

"You know, I have been thinking about some of our interactions in the past, and I bet if I were to start treating you less like a child and more like an adult, that we would have a better relationship. What do you think?"

I have a hard time imagining your teenager saying "No" to this. After their positive response, you might say something like:

"Great, and with my adult friends, I try to make sure that I listen and understand what's important to them, and expect that they will do that with me. This allows us to make adult-to-adult decisions. Does that work for you?"

Again, you should get a "Yes" from this, and this is important to ensure that you are checking in with them as you reset your relationship. You could then go on to say something like.

"Excellent, so, if, in the future, you feel that I'm not listening to you in a way you feel would be respectful, would you let me know, in a nice way, of course?"

They will, of course, say "Yes" to this, to which you can add:

"Great, and can I do the same with you, again in a nice way?"

It is very likely that they will also agree to this, albeit a little more reluctantly, because, while they are probably not thrilled at the prospect of your letting them know that they aren't listening in a caring way, the fact that you have framed this way of being as "what adults do," (and the fact that they want to be treated like an adult), should be enough to get their agreement.

So, now that you have checked one of the boxes that

represents a key to a teenager's cooperation, we can move to the second.

After they agree to all of the above, you can say something like:

"Great, and as a bonus, I anticipate this new relationship being good for you in other ways."

They should say, "What?" You say:

"Well, as we learn to trust each other more by listening and talking to each other in this more purposeful way, I imagine this will help me feel better about letting you do more things with your friends. Of course, I can't promise that I will always agree with you, but I can promise to listen and work hard to understand what is important to you and try to give you the benefit of the doubt. What do you think?"

They may jokingly say something like: "Who are you and what have you done with my mother / father?" However, even though they may be somewhat reluctant to believe that you are totally sincere (or that this isn't some sort of trick), because being treated like an adult, and trusted to make good decisions with their friends is so important to them, they are likely to want this to work.

Of course, this will have to be practiced and refined

as you go forward. However, the good news is that you will have laid a foundation of trust and respect with your teenager that has the real potential to turn into a loving, respectful, and trusting relationship with your grown children.

Section IV
Relationships

CHAPTER 27

What to Say...
When There are Problems
in Your Relationship

The Problem

Sadly, your relationship is not turning out the way you had hoped. There could be problems, such as, excessive fighting, a lack of communication, differences in parenting styles (or whether to have children at all), money issues, or a myriad of other problems, all that are making you wonder whether it is worth the effort.

What Not to Say...

Unfortunately, what most people do in these circumstances is try to convince their relationship partner to change. They remember how good things were "in the beginning," and try to get their partner to either stop something or start something so that it can be good again. It's almost as if what is binding the couple together is their love for each other and a memory of "how things were" when they were "in love," and, yet, all this does is put them in a position to hurt or be hurt.

The image I have is of two Roman gladiators bound together at their left wrists and forearms with rope. In their right hands, each holds a club and they just beat on each other until one of them dies!

I suggest that you don't sustain this sort of dysfunctional relationship.

A Top of the Mind Solution

Instead, create a platform that allows issues to be discussed without the conversation dissolving into a "who's right" debate. To do this, you speak not to what the other person is doing wrong, or how you want them to change, but to your vision of what you are looking for in a relationship. In fact, when working with couples, I start by helping them become clear about their individual visions (what they would want in any relationship). I then suggest that they share their visions with their partner to see where they match (or don't match).

The value of this approach is twofold. 1) When people are sharing their visions, there really isn't a right or wrong that needs to be debated, but just two people sharing what's important to them to see where there is agreement. 2) Because this is a conversation about the future (what you want in a relationship) versus the past, you are engaging the parts of the brain that think about the future, which are primarily the frontal lobes of the neocortex. This brings clarity to the conversation, and allows you and your relationship partner to come to the conclusion that either your visions are so different that this will never work, or that, while there may be differences, these are minor compared to the similarities.

What to Say…

One way of introducing this new way of dealing with conflict in a relationship might sound something like this:

"Honey, I have been thinking about all of the arguments we have had in the past, and I'm sure neither of us wants to continue down that road. Instead, I thought it would be a good idea for both of us to think about what we do want instead, and then see if we truly want the same things. Therefore, because I love you, I'm going to take a day or two and give some thought to what my vision of a relationship looks like. I hope you will do the same so that when we come back together, we can see where we stand and have more clarity about how to move forward."

Notice that this isn't asking permission to do this, or even insisting that they do the same thing. It's just you becoming clear about what you want to create in terms of a relationship (with anyone) going forward. This could include how you talk with each other, resolve disagreements, spend your time, share issues with friends and family, what your sex life looks like, how you raise your children (assuming that both of you want children), how you talk about money, religion, support each other in your careers (or lack thereof), etc.

The more complete, the better, however, it will be important to include those areas where there has been conflict in the past so that these issues don't get swept under the rug. Again, the reason this has the potential to be more successful is that you are talking about the future and what you want, versus how the other person needs to change.

Of course, this doesn't mean that one person can't change their vision if they choose to. For example, when I first met my wife, Georgia, and we were starting to get serious, she shared with me that being a mom and having kids was a big part of her vision of what she wanted in a relationship. At the time, I really didn't want kids, partly because I had grown up as an only child and didn't know how to deal with them, and partly because I thought you had to give up being a kid in order to have kids (in other words, become a "serious adult").

When I shared this with her, she very nicely told me that, while she understood my position, that she was not in the place in her life where she wanted to invest her time and energy in a relationship that was incongruent with her vision.

I was somewhat taken aback by this, however, after thinking about it for a while, I determined that the relationship was worth me changing my vision to match Georgia's in this area. What's important here is that Georgia didn't tell me that I had to or imply that what I wanted wasn't right. She just very clearly and lovingly told me what was important to her so that we could determine whether our visions were close enough to go forward.

Of course, if your relationship has dissolved to the

point where this sort of solution-focused conversation is difficult, or even impossible, you may want to engage a third party (a trained mental health professional) to help. Often, this is easier done in an atmosphere where you have engaged someone to help you stay focused on the future and what you want, versus how you are trying to get the other person to change.

If your partner just flatly refuses to engage in this sort of discussion altogether, you could write them a letter where you laid out your vision so at least they will know what you want going forward. Of course, if this is the case (your partner will not even talk with you about what you both want in a relationship going forward), this may be good information about whether you do indeed share the same vision, in which case, you may want to look at the next chapter… "What to Say When You Want to Break Up."

CHAPTER 28

What to Say...
When You Want to
Break Up

The Problem

Unfortunately, despite your best efforts, you have come to the realization that you and your partner want different things from a relationship. When this is the case, many people resort to trying to make the other person angry or upset so that they can use this conflict as a pretense for breaking up.

What Not to Say...

In these cases, people tend to focus on how the other person is wrong, with the ultimate goal of either their becoming so angry that they leave (so you don't feel guilty), or making them feel so bad that they agree that this relationship needs to end. Some will even start an affair so that when the other person learns of their infidelity, they will want to break up. None of these tactics are good ideas because they take whatever love and vulnerability that might still exist in the relationship and turn it into a weapon. This only makes the person you are breaking up with feel worse.

I also encourage you not to resort to the old line, "It's not you, it's me." I understand that this is meant to soften the blow of the breakup, however, it is rarely heard as good information, but rather some attempt to make them feel better about ending the relationship.

A Top of the Mind Solution

If you have taken my advice from the previous chapter and attempted to become clear about whether you and your relationship partner share the same vision, this can be the best place to start a conversation about breaking up. In this way, you aren't telling them that they are wrong or that they are the reason you are breaking up, but instead are focusing on the lack of congruence in your visions.

What to Say...

You could say something like:

"Honey, if there is one thing that has become clear, it's that we seem to want different things in a relationship. You have a perfect right to create the kind of relationship you want, as do I. It just seems as if we want different things. Therefore, as sad as this makes me feel, I'm going to move on."

Notice that this isn't about trying to convince them that this is the right thing to do or that they should agree with you. As an adult, you have the right (and the responsibility) to create a life that is congruent with what's important to you, and where you can be your authentic self.

In this communication, therefore, you aren't asking their permission to move on, or even needing them to agree that this is the right thing to do. Chances are that they won't! In fact, they may start arguing with you, telling you all the reasons you are wrong. If this is the case, I suggest you very lovingly say something like:

"Yes, I can understand that you see it that way, and… this is my decision."

Of course, if they are in a defensive or argumentative mood (which is understandable given what they are hearing), they are likely to attack this, as well. If so, you let them talk as long as they want (or as long as you are willing to listen), but rather than debating their arguments, you simply repeat,

"Yes, I can understand that you see it that way, and… this is my decision."

Pretty soon, they will get the message that you aren't going to argue with them or give them the opportunity to convince you to change your mind and give up. Of course, they are likely to still feel rejected and hurt, and this is something we can understand. However, because you know that ending a dysfunctional relationship is always the best thing for both people, you can take some comfort in the fact that you are freeing both of you to move on and hopefully create a more functional relationship with someone else.

Now, if there are children involved, this needs to be addressed in a way that reflects your love for them. Unfortunately, this may not be able to be done in the same conversation where you are breaking up with them, and so you might say something like:

"Of course, I know how much you love our kids, and the truth is, that while we may no longer be a couple, we will forever be their parents. My hope is that our love for them is stronger than our anger or resentment with each other, and that, in the future, we can show them how much we

love them by co-parenting in a very purposeful way."

I suggest that you leave it at that for the moment, because they are probably going to have to work through quite a bit of anger and resentment before they are able to access their love for your children in a way that supports your co-parenting relationship in the future.

The bottom line is that there is often no "good way" to break up if we define "good" as a conversation where both parties realize the fact that the relationship needs to end and chooses to do this in a loving manner. You are likely to feel guilty for making the other person feel bad, and they are likely to feel rejected and hurt. The truth is that there is a dream that is being shattered (the dream that you both had when you created the relationship) and it will take some time for both of you to grieve that shattered dream.

Plus, it's always harder on the person being left versus the person doing the leaving because they feel so out of control, especially if they don't want the relationship to end. Therefore, this isn't about how to make this sad situation feel good. It's about clarity with regard to the two factors that are necessary for a successful relationship (love and a common vision) and communicating with as much compassion as possible that one or both of these no longer exists in this relationship between you and your partner, and that you are moving on.

CHAPTER 29

What to Say... When Your Child (or Family Member) Comes Out to You as LGBTQ

The Problem

Chances are that this person has been wrestling with this issue for quite some time and may be worried about how you will react.

What Not to Say...

You don't want to respond by asking if this is something they have thought through, or are they sure? And, of course, trying to convince them that they are wrong is also a bad idea.

A Top of the Mind Solution

Instead, you want to let them know that you love them no matter what, and that you want them to be happy. Your love and acceptance will be a critical factor in their ability to love and accept themselves, and while this may not be the social stigma it was in the past, they will still very likely have a harder time than most going forward.

What to Say...

You could say something like:

"It means a lot to me that you would trust me with this information, and I want you to know that I will always love you and always want you to be happy. Tell me more about how you have come to this realization."

Here, you want to give them the opportunity to tell you their story as it relates to their identity, and your continued loving reaction (listening and empathizing, when appropriate) will be critically important to their ability to move forward feeling good about who they are and their self-worth.

I have members of my extended family who are gay, and they have asked me to encourage you to also include information on how to avoid AIDS, especially if the person coming out is gay or bisexual.

The information is as follows:

According to the Center For Disease Control (CDC) in 2015, "gay and bisexual men accounted for 82% (26,376) of new HIV diagnoses among all males aged 13 and older, and 67% of the total new diagnoses in the United States. Further, gay and bisexual men, aged 13 to 24, accounted for 92% of new HIV diagnoses among all men in their age group."

While AIDS isn't the death sentence it once was, these statistics show that being informed about how to prevent this disease could be critically important. Again, according to the CDC, "Pre-exposure prophylaxis, or PrEP, is a way for people who do not have HIV but who are at substantial risk of getting it to prevent HIV infection by taking a pill every day. The pill (brand name Truvada) contains two medicines (tenofovir and emtricitabine) that are used in combination with other medicines to treat HIV. When someone is exposed to HIV through sex or injection drug use, these medicines can work to keep the virus from establishing a permanent infection.

When taken consistently, PrEP has been shown to reduce the risk of HIV infection in people who are at high risk by up to 92%. PrEP is much less effective if it is not taken consistently. PrEP is a powerful HIV prevention tool and can be combined with condoms and other prevention methods to provide even greater protection than when used alone, however, people who use PrEP must commit to taking the drug every day and seeing their health care provider for follow-up appointments every three months."

All of this is to say that, in addition to providing social support for the person who is entrusting you with this information, giving them all the information they need to stay safe could also be a loving gesture on your part.

Of course, it's possible that this may be a bit much for the initial conversation. In other words, when someone is coming out to you, they are probably most concerned with your reaction versus looking for information on how to stay safe. Therefore, it might be a good idea to have the conversation on safety at another time. If so, you could start that conversation by saying something like,

"I want to thank you for trusting me enough to share your sexual (or gender) identity with me the other day. That meant a lot to me. And, you know I love you and want you to be safe. Would it be okay if we talked a bit about safety?"

Chances are that because you put it this way, they will be more open to this conversation than if you just started talking to them about all the things they should and shouldn't do to stay safe. Therefore, if they do indeed respond positively to your request, it might be a good idea to ask them about what they know first. For example, after they have given you permission to talk about safety, you could say:

"Great, have you heard about PrEP and how it can help prevent AIDS?"

Depending on what they say, you can either listen and fill in the blanks, or give them the complete picture based upon what you know. The challenge will be continuing to do this with all the love and compassion you have demonstrated to date.

Remember, their ability to accept themselves will be greatly impacted by your willingness to accept them. They have paid you a high compliment by sharing this information. If you can return that gift in a way that allows them to go into the world with confidence, this could make all the difference.

Section V
The Formula

CHAPTER 30

The LEAP Model, Or The "What to Say" Formula

The Problem

As you have seen, it's not uncommon for people to become worried, frustrated, and/or confused when confronted with a situation that they perceive to be a problem. Whether it has to do with our kids, our job, our family, or our relationships, this problematic perspective will tend to throw us into the problem-focused part of the brain (the lower brain) and limit our ability to know what to say or how to say it.

Therefore, what I have attempted to do in this book is give you information on how to avoid getting stuck in this limited and limiting part of the brain, and instead access the clarity, confidence, and creativity so necessary to engaging others successfully.

In my book, "Life from the Top of the Mind," I give readers a model for engaging others successfully that spells LEAP. I call it the LEAP Model because the steps not only spell "LEAP", but also because I believe that it will take somewhat of a "leap of faith" for us to become proficient at this way of communicating, given that few of us learned this information when we were young. I'm going to revisit some of this information here so that you have as much information as possible when dealing with others.

Let's begin by looking at the difference between being active or receptive when dealing with others who may be resistant to our message. This is important because, in order for any communication to go forward in a productive way, one person must be active and the other receptive. If two people are active, all you have is an argument. If two people are receptive, each is simply waiting for the other to make a decision.

Unfortunately, most of us have learned that the active role is the most powerful. Why? Because, as children, we experienced our parents and teachers actively telling us what to do while we were supposed to be receptive and listen to their directions. This taught us that powerful people are active and do the talking, while the less powerful (or even powerless) are supposed to listen and be receptive, and, thus, we resist this "receptive" position today because it seems powerless or less influential.

However, let's look at what is going on when we are dealing with someone who is being resistant. First, let's determine whether this (resistant) person is more likely to be active or receptive? Most would agree that these people are actively resisting what we have to say, and/or trying to convince us of something, and thus could accurately be described as being more active than receptive. So, what happens when they are active, and we respond by actively defending our position and/or try to convince them to change? You guessed it...they become even more resistant!

Therefore, while at some point, we do want to be able to bring our ideas into the conversation and have them heard as valuable information, to do this too soon will almost guarantee failure. Even if we are being "appropriately active," i.e., presenting our views in a calm, rational manner, if they are actively resisting or defending their own perspective, they will not hear what we have to say.

Of course, this is not to say that all people are like this. There may well be many people that come to you with a problem, you take the active role and give them the answer, and they happily go execute your instructions. In this case, the active role is very effective because the person is being receptive to your ideas and/or directions.

The problem is with those people who we might have labeled as "difficult" in the past, and who we now know to be simply stuck in the lower 20% of their brain. Because these people are being actively resistant, we must begin by being receptive if our goal is to become more influential.

When I suggest a receptive position with regard to these individuals, however, I am not just talking about becoming passive while they rant and rave. Neither am I suggesting that we just let them "vent" until they have "gotten it all out," and then tell them what we want them to know.

Instead, I suggest that we become very curious (a receptive, Top of the Mind quality) about what is driving their thoughts and emotions down into their lower brain so that we can eventually turn this information from the problem to part of the solution and motivate them to shift from their resistant brain to their receptive brain.

To be clear, I'm not just talking about tone of voice here, I am referring to all of the non-verbals (body language, facial expression, etc.) that influence how someone interprets what we are telling them. However, rather than becoming worried and/or stressed about whether our brows are knitted, or our arms are crossed in a "closed" position, all we really have to do is follow the first three steps in the LEAP model.

To help you accomplish this, I am going to identify five blocks that might be driving their resistance (or five ways their lower brain might be blocking their ability to engage in successful problem-solving), and how we might effectively respond to each.

Block/Driver # 1: They are, of course, very invested in the righteousness of their position, and very motivated to convince us that they are right. Their fear is that we won't listen, and that anything we say will be an effort to convince them that they are wrong. (This is why attempting to problem-solve or even get your point of view across at this point is fruitless, even if your solution is a good one.)

Suggestion: **Listen** and **Learn.** Listen, not to placate them or "just let them vent," but to discover (learn) the key to their cooperation (i.e. what they are worried about and/or what is important them). In other words, what is the belief/interpretation that is driving their lower brain reaction? Holding these questions in your mind should be helpful… What do they want you to know? What is most important to them as an outcome? The best way to discover these keys is to listen to what they are saying without needing to counter their logic or their position. Here are a few questions that you can ask:

- *What are you most concerned about here?*
- *What do you want me to know about this situation?*

And/or...

- *What is most important to you here?*

The important thing to remember is that you are gathering data about what is driving their lower brain reaction, not engaging in a debate about who's right. I would also suggest that you listen in a way that would allow you to paraphrase what you heard, if necessary.

Of course, listening and paraphrasing are pretty standard communication tools, however, I am suggesting that you use them in different ways than most books on communication or conflict resolution. For example, I am not suggesting that you listen and paraphrase simply to allow the other person to feel "understood." Instead, I'm suggesting that you draw your motivation to listen from your desire to discover their driver, or the key to their cooperation, so that you can harness that energy, and, at some point, become more influential in the interaction.

In addition, I'm not even suggesting that you need

to paraphrase everything you hear, especially if this comes in the form of just repeating what they say. For example, when someone tells you that they are feeling angry and frustrated, I am not suggesting that you then say, "I hear you are feeling angry and frustrated." Chances are they will interpret this as some technique you read in a book and will very likely become even more resistant as a result. I am suggesting that you listen so that you could paraphrase, if necessary.

This is a very different form of listening than most of us practice, especially in a situation where there is potential disagreement. Listening so that you could paraphrase is closer to how we listen to directions when getting to some destination as soon as possible is our priority.

For example, let's assume that we are lost on a country road, and we are trying to get to a lake house where our friends and family are waiting on us for dinner. We stop a local and ask directions, and he says:

"The old Crawford place? Sure, I know where that is. You just go on down this road until you see a big tree on your right. Then you turn left and go, say, about a mile or two until you see a pond on your left, and turn right. You then keep on going until the road goes over a big hill, and you will come to a fork in the road, and that's where you turn left. After that, you just look for a grove of trees with a house in the middle, and that's the place. You can't miss it!"

Hmmmmm... At this point, because this is very valuable information and we want to make sure we heard it correctly, we might say, "Okay, let me get this straight. You go down this road . . ." In other words, we would paraphrase what we heard to check for accuracy, because if we don't get it right, we won't be able to get to where we want to go!

This is exactly how and why we want to listen to the resistant person with whom we may be having a conversation, because what they are telling us is very valuable information about where they are, and this information will be critical to our getting where we want to go with them, (i.e., motivating them to shift to the more rational part of their brain and willingly participating in the problem-solving process).

Plus, if you remember, one of their concerns is that we won't listen, and thus they may challenge us at some point by saying something like: "You haven't heard a word I have said, have you!!?" If we have been listening in this very specific way, we can say, "Well, what I have heard so far is _____. Did I get it right?" This will not only allay one of their fears (that we're not listening), it will also allow us to check to see if we interpreted what we heard accurately, which again is very important if we plan to use this information later in the discussion

In addition, there is another reason to listen in such a way that you can paraphrase. It's very common for people who are stuck in their lower brain to go off on rants and tangents that seem to have no real connection to the original problem. They may say one or two things that are meaningful, and then go off into the wild blue yonder on some third issue that no one can do anything about. If you are listening so that you can paraphrase, this is your opportunity to interrupt them and redirect the conversation in the only way they will allow.

For example, with most people, if they sense that you are wanting to interrupt them to counter their position, they will very likely resist. You can say, "But, but, but..." all day long, trying to get a word in edgewise, and they will try just as hard to keep on talking, because the word, "but" signals that you are wanting to counter what they just said.

However, if you say something like, "Okay, let me make sure I'm getting this right..." or even, "I don't want to forget what you said earlier. Could you tell me more about…," they are going to be much more willing to let you interrupt them because they are invested in you getting it right. Plus, at this point, you can paraphrase what you heard them say on the first two pertinent points (leaving out the tangent) and ask them to tell you more about these issues. You will be amazed at how this refocuses the conversation on the more germane information and moves the process along at the same time.

Block/Driver # 2: They are afraid that we don't get it, that we don't understand their position, or that we believe they shouldn't be (or have no valid reason to be) so upset. Or, they are simply afraid that we think they are wrong and are about to tell them so. So, what can we do? How can we respond in a way that allows them to stop defending their perspective, and/or their right to be resistant?

Suggestion: **Empathize**: I know, this can sound like psychobabble, so let me explain. By "empathize," I don't mean that you need to "feel their pain," hold their hand, or become their counselor. In fact, this step, while essential, takes only a few seconds, and could be accomplished as easily as saying something like, "I can see how you would be upset by this." Or, "I can see how this would be important to you."

Many people have trouble with this concept because they are afraid that in order to empathize with someone's position (or why they might be upset), they must agree with them. The important thing to remember here is that:
Understanding doesn't necessarily mean agreement!

It just means that, given what we now know about how negative beliefs can drive someone into their lower brain, we can see how they might be resistant or upset.

For example, imagine that you are dealing with a person who is angry because he believes that he has been treated unfairly in some way. If you were to say, "I don't know where you are getting this. You are being treated just like everyone else!," he would most likely become even more resistant, and redouble his efforts to defend his position. If, on the other hand, you said something like, "I can see how you would be upset by that," it wouldn't mean that you agreed with him. It would simply mean that, you can understand how someone would be upset if he or she feels that they are being treated unfairly.

What's most important, however, is that empathizing with someone will allow them to give up the need to defend their position, and, thus, they would be more open to what you have to say next. This leads us to the third block to effective communication, and yet another driver of their lower brain reaction.

Block/Driver # 3: They are afraid that we are going to blame them for something they did or said in the past, or that we are going to use the past in some way to prove our point. This concern is understandable because, in the past, I'm sure that most of the people with whom they have disagreed have indeed argued with them about who's right.

However, this is also where we can become more influential in that we are not going to respond like "most people." In fact, now that we have information about what is important to them gathered in Step One (Listen/Learn) and used Step Two (Empathize) to defuse their need to defend their position, we can now begin to encourage them then to shift from their lower brain up into the upper brain.

Suggestion: **Ask A Top of the Mind Question.** In my book, Life from the Top of the Mind, I describe how questions can exert a powerful influence over what part of the brain we are in. Unfortunately, in the past, many of us have found ourselves asking lower brain questions (or BS questions) when dealing with a resistant person. These could include questions that run through our mind such as, "What is wrong with this person? Can't they see how stupid they are being? Why won't they listen to reason? How could they do/think such a thing?" etc.)

As you can see, questions such as these will throw us into the lower 20% of our brain and limit our ability to be effective. Further, resistant people are also likely to be asking themselves lower brain questions about us. For example, they may be thinking, "Who do they think they are? Why won't they listen to me?

Why do I always have to defend myself with this person? Can't they understand that my perspectives or beliefs are just as valid as theirs?"

Therefore, given that the lower brain is not where you want to be or where you want them to be, I suggest that you instead become curious and "**Listen** and **Learn**" what is important to them, **Empathize** so that they no longer need to defend their position, and then **Ask "Top of the Mind questions."** Top of the Mind questions are almost always questions about the future and the solution, versus the problem and the past.

Why? Because, almost every discussion involving conflict is about who did what in the past. Unfortunately, this will be a fruitless debate, because they will remember it one way while you will remember it another, and both of you will be trying to prove the other wrong. Therefore, one benefit of asking a question about the future is that at least we are now discussing what will be, versus what was, and the discussion is no longer about "who's to blame."

Of course, these will differ slightly depending on the type of situation you are dealing with. This is why I have attempted to give you as many examples as possible, and why this book is called, *What to Say*. Basically, it is about what sorts of Top of the Mind questions will help people shift to their receptive brain and hear what you have to say as valuable.

To review, we have learned that, listening, empathizing and asking Top of the Mind questions are critical steps in dealing with people when they are being resistant. What you may or may not have noticed, however, is that all of these steps are receptive in nature. This is what I mean when I say that when dealing with conflict, it is the receptive position that is initially the most powerful.

Plus, these steps change the color of the interaction in a way that makes the last step, **problem-solving**, more successful. In other words, our willingness to practice these receptive skills will not only give us valuable information about the key to their cooperation and allow them to shift from their lower brain to their Top of the Mind, it will gradually reduce the "us versus them" nature of the conflict and allow them to see us less as an adversary, and more as an ally.

Of course, at some point, we are going to want to take an active position if our goal is to be influential with this person. I just want to caution against going to the active step of problem-solving too soon, i.e., before you know the key to their cooperation, and/or before they have shifted from the lower brain to the Top of the Mind.

How will you know if it's too soon? They will balk

at your solution. This could come in the form of a "Yes, but...," or "I tried that and it didn't work," or some other statement that lets us know that the real key to their cooperation, or what's really important to them, is missing in the solution we offered. If this happens, the challenge will be to see this response as "good information" (versus a problem that will engage our lower brain), and repeat steps 1-3 (Listen/Learn, Empathize, Ask) to determine what we missed.

Of course, I'm not suggesting that you simply continue to repeat steps one through three ad nauseam. Instead I suggest you determine how many times you are willing to go back to listening to see what you missed. As for myself, I will do this up to three times. If after my third attempt to understand what is important to them, empathize, and ask a Top of the Mind question, they are still balking at moving into problem-solving, I will suggest we take some time to think about the situation.

This might sound something like this,

Okay, I can see how this is important to you, and I would like some time to give your concerns more thought to see what can be done. How about we both give this some thought and meet again (later today, tomorrow, etc.)?

I would encourage you to set a specific time to meet

so that this doesn't get forgotten or swept under the rug. I also suggest that this next meeting be fairly soon (say within 24 or 48 hours). What I have noticed is that after a short time has passed, both parties (us and them) return having thought about the situation in a way that leads to a solution.

Just remember, even if this is a new conversation, when we go to problem-solving, we will need to bring all that we learned from the first three steps into this last stage, and blend this information (what's important to them and what's important to us) in a very purposeful manner.

One final tip... remember to use the magic word "and" versus "but" as a transition from the empathizing step to the step where we are asking Top of the Mind questions. For example, many people have learned that it's a good idea to acknowledge what another says before they offer their own opinion. Unfortunately, when this is done using the word "but" as the transition, it will likely fail, because "but" negates whatever comes before it.

For example, imagine during a disagreement that someone says this to you, "Yes, I hear what you're saying, BUT..." Chances are that you will not be eager to hear what comes next because your position was negated with the word "but." It's like going up to a member of your organization and saying, "Sally, you have really been doing a great job, BUT ..." The words "you are doing a great job" are immediately negated by the word "but," and thus the person with whom you are wanting to communicate will not be inclined to appreciate what you have to say next.

Instead, use the word "and." For example, "I hear what you are saying, AND I have some ideas about the situation as well." This allows people to be more open to what you are about to say because you have not negated what they just said. In fact, you have set up a situation where you can draw from what they think/believe/want, and what is important to you in crafting a solution. This increases the potential that your solution will be heard in a positive light because you have included something that's important to them.

This is especially true when you are in a position of leadership or authority and wanting to correct someone's behavior. In fact, thinking of "correcting" this person's behavior in terms of, "How can my solution be valuable in helping them get what they want?" is an excellent way to conceptualize how you might want to frame your suggestion for change. Or, put another way:

The most effective form of correction is when the other feels informed versus chastised.
As mentioned, this model, which is designed to

help resistant individuals shift from their lower brain to their Top of the Mind spells LEAP (Listen/ Learn, Empathize, Ask (Top of the Mind questions,) and Problem-solve). It will indeed take a "leap of faith" for us to become skilled at this way of dealing with others, and therefore, I encourage you to give yourself some time to become comfortable with the process.

Also, I encourage you to use the power of your imagination to see yourself going through the steps with people within your mind before you try it in person. In fact, you may not want to try this on the most difficult person you know at first. Starting with less intense interactions and working your way up to those individuals who have been especially prob-lematic in the past would be a better idea.

Of course, I do know that there are people who are so frightened (or stuck in their lower brain) that we can LEAP with them all day long and it won't make any difference. However, I suggest that even with these people, the LEAP model is the best way to respond if your goal is to maximize success. Why? Well, for one thing, the LEAP model doesn't give them anything negative to complain about. The interesting thing about "difficult people" is that if we were to ask them who are the difficult people in their lives, they would probably say us! They see our past reaction to them as the problem, and may even use this reaction to justify, or even intensify their original resistant behavior.

However, when we are able to deal with them by listening/learning, empathizing, asking, and then problem-solving, we don't give them any "ammunition" to fire back at us or complain about. What are they going to say... "They just listened to me too much?" or "They were too interested in what I had to say?"

Unlikely. Plus, even if they don't change, we can be very proud of our part of the conversation, and are, therefore, less likely to "take on their stuff" or leave the conversation feeling frustrated or resentful.

Recently, I have expanded this model to include two additional blocks or obstacles to effective communication and influence (that occur prior to our using the LEAP Model), and an antidote to each. The first is our state of mind. As I'm sure you know, when we are stressed, frustrated, annoyed or even simply tired and drained, we will not be in the "Top of the Mind," and as a result, will not have access to the sort of interpersonal skills and problem-solving skills that are necessary to deal with difficult people. In addition, our stress, frustration, and resentment are likely to leak into our nonverbals (tone of voice, body language, etc.) and this may have them hearing "you stupid idiot" on the end of what we say.

The antidote to this is being very clear about our highest purpose, or the qualities and characteristics we want to bring to the interaction (for example, clear, confident, creative, compassionate, etc)... and, being willing to bring these to life, regardless of how they are being (remember, we never want to tie our piece of mind to their state of mind).

The second block or obstacle to effective communication and influence is our trying to stop their negative behavior, or seeing them as just being resistant, argumentative, or stubborn. Now, we know that this is only who they are when they are stuck in the lower 20% of the brain. Instead, I suggest you focus not on what you want them to stop, but what you want them to start.

In other words, you know who they are when they are coming from their lower brain. What you want to find out is who are they when they are coming from their Top of the Mind. Have you ever seen them exhibiting the sort of qualities you are looking for? Has there ever been a time in the past when you saw them being open-minded, curious, helpful, or whatever you would like them to be with you now? If so, try to hold an image of them at their best, because that is what you want to bring out.

The LEAP Model completes the next four steps

(Listen/Learn, Empathize, Ask, and Problem-solve), and puts all the information we have learned so far together to create a six-step process to minimize resistance and maximize communication and co-operation.

Okay, now you know the science and the formula behind all of the suggestions in this book. Again, I want to emphasize that I'm not saying these are the only ways to become influential with others or that you should say things exactly the way I do. I just wanted to give you my best thoughts on how you can become more influential with others.

There is a quote that I use in almost all of my seminars and books that is from Albert Einstein. He said,

"Problems cannot be solved at the same level of awareness that created them."

Therefore, my goal in writing this book was to help you raise your awareness of the science behind why people can be resistant to what we have to say (lower brain versus Top of the Mind) and give you as many examples as possible of how to engage others in a way that minimizes misunderstandings and maximizes solution-focused conversations that are beneficial to all concerned.

That being said, it would have been impossible to cover all scenarios, and, therefore, for those of you who have purchased this book in any form, I want to say thanks by offering to give my best thoughts on what to say in your specific situation. In other words, if none of the examples described in this book truly apply to your situation, feel free to go my website (www.BillCrawfordPhD.com), send me an email and I will be happy to give you my best thoughts on "What To Say" in your specific situation.

You can also go to my YouTube channel (just Google Bill Crawford, Ph.D. YouTube) and check out my videos to learn more about how my "Life from the Top of the Mind" can be applied to a variety of situations. I have been posting one each week for several years, and at this writing, have over 300 available.

At the end of each video, I sign off with a wish for my viewers. I say, "Here's to you bringing more clarity, confidence, and creativity to everything you do, and I will look forward to seeing you in the future." I wish the same for you.

www.ingramcontent.com/pod-product-compliance
Lightning Source LLC
Chambersburg PA
CBHW030011290326
41934CB00005B/294